Norse Shamanism

Secrets of Nordic Shamanic Rituals, Beliefs, Magic, Herbalism, and Practices

Free Bonus from Silvia Hill available for limited time

Hi Spirituality Lovers!

My name is Silvia Hill, and first off, I want to THANK YOU for reading my book.

Now you have a chance to join my exclusive spirituality email list so you can get the ebooks below for free as well as the potential to get more spirituality ebooks for free! Simply click the link below to join.

P.S. Remember that it's 100% free to join the list.

~~$27~~ FREE BONUSES

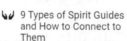 9 Types of Spirit Guides and How to Connect to Them

 How to Develop Your Intuition: 7 Secrets for Psychic Development and Tarot Reading

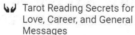 Tarot Reading Secrets for Love, Career, and General Messages

Access your free bonuses here
https://livetolearn.lpages.co/norse-shamanism-paperback/

Table of Contents

Introduction

Norse Shamanism is a religion with practitioners believing in a raw spirituality that differs from many other ancient practices. It is a religion that honors the elements of fire, water, earth, and air. It's been said that "The gods dwell within the rocks themselves." The story of the gods is told through an oral tradition, with brazen spirituality that isn't just a romantic idea of a lost people but a way of life that modern-day practitioners can still experience.

Norse Shamanism is a religious system practiced in Northern Europe for thousands of years. It involves a journey to the world of spirits held in the highest regard. Shamans walk between the worlds and become immersed in the spiritual realm. Their role is as both healer and medium, healing the body while communicating with ancestor spirits. The shaman travels from this world to the spirit world through a trance or an ecstatic experience, which is almost always brought on by drumming, rattling, and dancing.

Popular media often portray the Norse as bloodthirsty people who waged war on anyone who dared step foot into their territory, but this is far from accurate. The beliefs of the Norse people were a lot more complex than that. They saw their land as the center of the universe, and all other lands beyond it stretched forth from there. The Norse culture and myths are a rich source to draw from since humans at the time of its beginning were so in touch with nature. They were deeply spiritual people who lived on the fringe of the known world. They thrived when left alone but became fierce when provoked. This duality is evident in their complex rituals, many of which involved animal sacrifices. However, they believed it was wrong to kill an animal without reason, so they would only do so in times of need.

This book will guide modern-day shamans to connect with the spirit world and learn more about the culture of the ancient Norse. It will delve into the mysterious Northern beliefs and rituals while explaining the truths behind them. In this way, it can guide people who practice Shamanism in the 21st century and who want to learn more about their ancestors. The rituals and beliefs are all found in ancient texts and are clearly explained here so that people can understand them intellectually.

The book will focus on the practical aspects of becoming a Norse shaman with exercises and rituals to try out yourself. It will awaken the shamanic powers within you and show you how to use them in your everyday life. It is also a tool for students of the occult who are sincerely interested in Norse Shamanism. Here you'll find insights into the beliefs and rituals of shamans from ancient times, how to recreate what they did, and learn more about their philosophy and worldview.

Chapter One: Norse Shamanism Basics

A Shaman is a person who can communicate with different realms and dimensions, as well as creatures that reside there. They are spiritual healers who use different rituals and practices to physically and spiritually heal people and their environments. The shaman is an intermediary between worlds and must be able to see and interact with all these realms, people, and creatures. This means a close relationship exists between the shaman and the spirit world. They heal afflictions through several spiritual practices, ranging from purification rituals to exorcisms, from counseling sessions to incantations. Not only that, but the shaman also creates sacred objects and symbols (i.e., tattoos, totems) and has knowledge of special magic plants that provide protection, health, fertility, and longevity.

Shamanism is an ancient spiritual practice passed down through generations in many cultures and locations. It is the state of being entirely connected with nature and everything that exists. This includes other living beings, the planets and stars, past, present, and future thoughts, and all life forms, including non-physical. The shaman is thought to be in a non-ordinary reality where they can communicate with other beings and spirits to obtain healing or knowledge. They use their connection with the spirit world to cure spiritual, emotional, and physical problems within a community.

Origins of Shamanism

The history of shamanic magic extends back to the Paleolithic period, approximately 2.5 million years ago, up to 10,000 BC in Europe and Asia. There are cave paintings that depict human figures wearing animal masks, ornamented with necklaces and crowns made from animal teeth and claws. Shamans were spirit-workers who served various functions, such as healers and spiritual guides, for their society. They were spiritual healers, teachers, and navigators of the spirit world.

Shamans are considered experts in a particular trade or profession in many cultures. They are sacred figures, being regarded as conduits to the spirit world. Shamans create and utilize a sacred space in which ordinary reality, the spiritual world, and our individual spirits are all placed on an equal playing field. The shaman can utilize different states of consciousness to reach what we'd commonly refer to as the "supernatural," meaning that they can access things that are not visible to the average person. By doing so, a shaman may be able to find solutions to problems by traveling into the spirit world, where they may meet with other spirits. The word "shaman" comes from the Tungusic people of Siberia, considered one of the earliest recorded cultures with knowledge of this practice. The term derives from the Tungus word "Shingmak," meaning "to be gifted or possessing a special power."

The Magico-Religious Aspects of Shamanism

There are several types of shamans, and they perform a variety of roles. Some people adhere to a more formalized system, with certain roles and ceremonies passed down from generation to generation. Others have more fluid systems in that various practitioners have different levels of knowledge and perform different functions. Some shamans are healers, some are guides for others who have lost their way, some predict coming events and others go into spirit realms to interact with the other world inhabitants, depending on their individual skills and preferences.

Shamanism teaches that the spirit world exists on a parallel plane of reality, which is not bound by time and can occur anywhere. Shamans can interact with the spirits of their ancestors, living and dead, often going into trances to travel to different locations. The shaman may also travel through time, meeting and interacting with the spirits of the past and future.

Shamanism is often thought of as a rational practice with few elements that are purely magical or mystical. The word "magico-religious" describes Shamanism as both magic and as a religion. Shamanism combines spirituality, magic, worship, and religious rites in one single practice. This means some rituals are a mixture of magical practices and religious aspects.

Norse Shamanism

The practice of Shamanism found its way to Northern Europe thanks to the nomadic tribes who migrated there. Shamanism greatly affected these people and may have even influenced Nordic society to adopt some of their practices. Shamans were extremely important for a nomadic society such as this. They would have been able to reach decisions through dialogue with the spirits on what was best for the community. Depending on what the spirits told them, they could determine whether it was best to migrate north or south, east or west.

The Norse spent much of their time traveling from place to place, but when they settled down in Iceland around 900 A.D., they developed a more formalized system for practicing shamanic magic and spirit worship. In Scandinavia, there were two types of shamans; the "sorcerer" and the "witch." The sorcerer was a person who had training in magic and rune-casting (an art very similar to alchemy in the Middle Ages). It was his role to deal with spirits and nature. The witch was a female shaman who could heal the sick or predict important events. The Norse also believed that the spirits of their ancestors were still very much a part of life and that these ancestral spirits could come back in the form of an animal a person may encounter. They called this a "transformation," meaning that a spirit could enter into an animal to bring about change or implement healing work. In terms of spirit allies, the Norse were known to be in touch with many spirits, some helpful and some not. Perhaps one of the most famous spirits to visit these people was Odin, who was known to be able to shape-shift into a variety of different animals. Odin would often appear to people in the form of a cat, an owl, or a raven. He was even known to take these forms in battle and to aid the Norse when performing magic and rituals.

Difference between Norse Shamanism and Other Forms of Shamanism

Runelore. What makes the Norse religion unique is its belief in the power of runes and its elaboration on the magic of the runes. Never before had someone documented so much about a particular magical system as the Vikings did. The reason for this was that the Norse were great record keepers, and many of their runic writings have been preserved for us to read today. The runes were believed to contain a mysterious power that came from Odin. They were thought to contain unique energy which could be manipulated by a skilled rune caster or practitioner who understood their meaning. In addition to acting as a magical tool, runes were also viewed as symbolic or representational of physical quality. If a person carved the rune Fehu into an object, it would bring good luck to that object and represent goodness and protection.

Runes have their origin in the pre-Christian Nordic society. Before runes were used for writing on paper and stone, they were used in sorcery, divination, and chanting. In the ancient world, runes were carved onto ritual objects for magical purposes, such as curing diseases or influencing people's lives in many ways. The runes could represent the person and their actions. They could also represent a divine or spiritual force that would work on the person and a spiritual force that would work directly on another person. For instance, the runic symbol "Gebo" represented gift-giving and marriage. It was used for engagement gifts and for other purposes related to weddings. A couple would carve Gebo into their possessions to protect their relationship from harm.

All of these different uses for the rune were aspects of Norse shamanism, which included the forging of objects and the making of talismans to bring about protection through magical means. It also included casting magical spells and the creation of amulets to ward off evil spirits or protect a person from death. It was believed that if one carried a runic amulet made by a shaman, they would be under the protection of powerful spirits, including Odin. The Vikings were known to make objects containing runes that could bring safety and protection during their journeys. These objects were believed to house powerful spirits (archetypes) within them—spirits that could come out during rituals or war. These types of sorcery practices survived in some Nordic traditions through the Middle Ages. No records of any other shamanic practice exhibited this type of magical behavior.

Seidr. Another interesting aspect of the Norse was their practice of Seidr. Seidr is a form of sorcery, but it can also be viewed as a type of shamanic practice. Like the runes, seidr comes from Nordic origins and means "to bewitch." It is believed that seidr was taught by Odin and passed down to the human race. It can be used for various purposes, including healing, foretelling the future, finding out what happened in the past, and contacting the dead. In fact, seidr was used to contact the spirits of ancestors so they could pass on important information, such as how to cure a disease or live a better life. This form of magic can be accomplished through meditation or trance-like states where the practitioner communes with spirits or deities to gain their favor or to learn how to perform magic.

In ancient Nordic society, seidr was an essential part of their culture and traditions. It was used by women who were called "volva." These individuals would commune with spirits and deities to predict the future, find out about events that were going on elsewhere, or contact specific entities. However, a woman who practiced seidr was not necessarily a witch. She was more of a fully-fledged shaman because her training included spirit travel and other types of shamanic practices.

It is said that the volva often experienced great pain and fatigue while they were in a trance. They would often knock their heads against the ground to purge negative energy, just as shamans did. Their trance would lead them into an altered state of consciousness where they could see the "otherworld" and communicate with spirits. Through this ability, they could learn how to cast spells or perform incredible feats of magic. Sometimes, they would even have the ability to transform themselves into animals.

Despite the beliefs surrounding a woman who practiced seidr, nothing about her was evil or malicious. She was often called upon by people who had difficult problems and needed spiritual guidance, especially if it came from an ancestor. The presence of a volva during this time was considered a privilege, and she was treated with great respect because she could help people in various ways—ways that most other people couldn't.

Although Seid workers were primarily women, men could sometimes perform the same functions as a volva. A male said the worker was called a "seiðmaðr," and they were also called upon to contact spirits and could put themselves into a trance to do so, but they were less prevalent than their female counterparts and were even considered feminine. This is because the spiritual skills involved with seidr were associated with womanly qualities, such as being emotional and intuitive.

Berserkergang. The Norse had another form of Shamanism known as berserkergang, which involved spirit possession and rage. During berserkergang, a person would enter an altered state of consciousness and become extremely violent and uncontrollable. They would typically act out like a possessed warrior and would lose all control over their thoughts and feelings. Berserkers were people who practiced berserkergang, and this practice was limited to people who belonged to the Norse culture.

Berserkergang was a religious practice used by the Vikings to bring about spiritual transformation through various means, including magic or shamanic practices. This type of spirituality was important during the Viking age and was used during ritualistic practices. These practices often involved making sacrifices to the deities or the spirits who lived around them and consuming special herbal brews.

During berserkergang, people were said to have felt no pain and were able to heal wounds very quickly—a gift that is commonly attributed to shamans by people who adhere to shamanic practices even today. During this time, they would bite their shields and cut themselves with their swords without being harmed at all. This was a trance state where the person was in complete union with the spirits, and the violence they felt was actually a language they could speak.

Berserkergang's purpose was religious, but it could also be used in times of conflict or to prepare warriors before battle. The practice of berserkergang allowed people to learn how to use their bodies and emotions to overcome their adversaries. Warrior practices taught that the human body was like a wolf pack—a pack that consisted of five animals; a bear, boar, bull, cat, and an eagle. These animals represented a metaphor for the five characteristics which people should have to survive; speed, strength, cunning, reflexes, and stamina. These characteristics were not only necessary to survive in the wilderness, but they were also necessary when it came to war.

Through berserkergang, a person gained the ability to transform into one of these animals, which would allow them to fight and kill their enemies quickly and efficiently. They would also learn how to heal themselves in a battle to continue fighting despite injuries. Today's version of these practices is known as martial arts. However, one must be careful not to confuse this with berserkergang because it does not include aspects associated with spirit-possession or trance states.

Practicing Norse Shamanism Today

Although the practice of Norse shamanism is not as common as it was during the time of the Vikings, it is still a recurring phenomenon. Today, many people believe in the practice of Norse shamanism and continue to hold on to its beliefs. There are also practitioners of Norse shamanism who prefer to keep their beliefs a secret and protect them at all costs. Because of this, it can be difficult for those who practice these traditions to find others who share their beliefs.

Although Norse Shamanism became more mainstream during the 20th century, it can still be lost among other types of spirituality because of the language in which it is expressed. Many people are confused about whether modern-day practitioners of seidr actually know what a seid worker was and the conditions in which they lived. As a result, many believe that they can incorporate nationalistic elements into their practice and turn it into something else.

This is unfortunate because when someone uses this type of spirituality to indulge in their own agenda, they can cause harm to other people. To prevent this from happening, we must be honest with ourselves and realize there is no way to re-invent these traditions because they already existed thousands of years ago. We must maintain the integrity of this type of spirituality or risk corrupting it entirely. In the 21st century, it is essential to remember two things when practicing Norse Shamanism:

1. It is vital to understand that these are religious practices that have been passed down through history and,

2. It is important to recognize their role in the past and how they affect us today.

Can Anyone Become a Shaman?

As it is with many other types of spirituality, anyone can become a shaman, but, to do this, you must have the patience and endurance to practice the art. You must have the desire and the discipline to maintain a connection with the spirits. You also need to respect the deities who will help you along your path.

There are several ways to become a shaman, but there is no definite answer as to how to do this. Some people go through apprenticeships, some go through cold-calling, and others go in search of signs from the gods and goddesses. Regardless of which method you choose, you must remain focused and recognize that achieving this goal requires a lot of hard work and dedication. To practice some forms of Shamanism like seidr, you must find someone who will teach you everything you need to know about the practice and explain it in a way you can understand.

The best way to achieve this goal is to look at it as a quest. In many ways, the shaman is similar to a knight—they are often seen as heroes who fight for others and help them overcome their obstacles. To begin your quest, you must start by searching for guidance using your higher self. Ask yourself the hard questions. How do you feel about other religions? How do you feel about the deities? Where do you see yourself in your future? What is important to you? Are you ready for this? Only when you are honest with yourself can you really find out what you want in life and the best way to obtain it. Once you have asked yourself these questions, listen to your higher self as it begins to open up a pathway for you. Follow this path and discover the true power that lies within.

Chapter Two: The Nine Realms of the Tree of Life

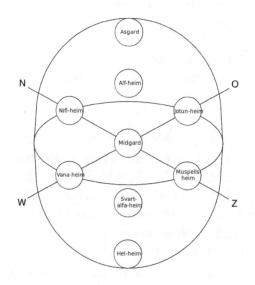

The nine realms of the tree of life.
Et2brute, CC0, via Wikimedia Commons:
https://commons.wikimedia.org/wiki/File:Nine_Realms.svg

To the Norse, Yggdrasil is a massive tree that they believe holds together the Nine Worlds. It's not just looked at as having a spiritual representation but literally holding all the worlds together. It's considered the root of their faith but can also represent spiritual energy, health, and life. The tree is believed to be self-regenerating, with the ability to give life to everything that exists on it.

Yggdrasil (pronounced eegh-dra-seel) is often translated as "World Tree" or "Tree of Life." The name is derived from the Old Norse words "Ygg," meaning "Terrifier" or "Odin," and "drasil," meaning "horse." The tree is believed to be an Ash, a type of tree that grows in Northern Europe. Its branches reach out to each of the Norse worlds and connect them together. A well lies beneath the tree, where it's believed the original man, Ymir, was formed before being killed by Odin and his brothers Vili and Ve. He was then used as the base to create all the realms, except for Muspelheim and Niflheim, which already existed.

Shamans are thought to possess an extraordinary ability to enter into altered states of consciousness to communicate with or travel between these realms. In fact, shamans believe that these realms are so interconnected that they share a common space, which can be accessed by individuals with the ability to journey through the gates of reality. Those who lack this skill can be taught how to perform this by following certain rituals and being trained by more experienced shamans. The journey is thought to be difficult because of the possibility of never being able to find your way back.

Yggdrasil

The Norse Tree of Life wasn't always a tree. In the beginning, it was said to have been a magical well where Ymir, the first living being in existence, was molded from its waters. After his death, the first god, Odin, is said to have thrown Ymir's skull up into the sky, where it became the heavens. His blood became the ocean, his flesh became the Earth, and his hair, the grasses of the field.

Ymir's body parts were thrown in different directions, forming the realms and other elements as we know them today. The magic well that started it all was placed at the center of everything, where the root of it all, Yggdrasil, begins. It is within this tree that all nine worlds communicate and connect with one another. While Yggdrasil supports all things, it's said to have a vulnerability in that if it were ever cut down or destroyed, everything holding up Nine Worlds would collapse as well. For this reason, the gods dread the coming of Ragnarok, the end of the world, when Yggdrasil will be struck and destroyed, but with a new world being born from the ashes.

The Norse believe that everything contains a smaller version of itself within it, which is why Yggdrasil is said to be an Ash tree, a type of tree known for regrowing from its own ashes when burned. The tree isn't only a physical representation of the cycle of life but also a spiritual representation. This belief is reinforced through myths about the first humans being formed from an ash tree, and from the tree, they obtained wisdom and understanding. The sap from the Ash tree is also believed to contain unique healing properties, which are used to help ease pain or cure diseases. Throughout history, rituals involving Ash trees have been conducted for thousands of years by different cultures worldwide for different purposes, including to ease grief and in the hope of helping the dying transition into the afterlife.

The Nine Worlds of Norse Cosmology

The Nine Worlds are believed to be a collection of nine planes or dimensions in Norse mythology. They are:

- Asgard
- Midgard (the world we live on)
- Vanaheim
- Jotunheim
- Niflheim
- Helheim
- Nidavellir
- Muspelheim
- Alfheim

Each of these worlds is thought to have its own characteristics and is represented by different things such as mountains and animals or specific natural elements such as Muspelheim being of fire or Nidavellir, which is described as having its own time.

The Nine Worlds are not considered to be separate dimensions. Instead, they are thought to be different parts of one realm that we can visit. They represent everything that exists in this world and how the universe works on a macroscopic level. They represent how complex and interconnected everything is, with the gods having their hands in every detail and using the elements to create and sustain everything in existence. Let's look at some distinctive details about each realm.

Asgard

Asgard is the realm where the Aesir clan of gods is said to live. It is a land filled with endless beauty, joy, and happiness that is said to stretch out to the nine realms. However, this paradise has its own vulnerabilities. Without the Aesir clan's involvement, all of the Nine Worlds would die and, in doing so, would collapse into one another resulting in eternal darkness and nothingness where no one could ever exist. This is why they are known as gods and possess such great power over their creations. The Aesir clan is protected by Odin, who leads them into battle against enemies and offers them victory against the onslaught of chaos that comes from the realm of darkness that resides at their side in a place called Niflheim.

Asgard is further divided into large homes known as Gladsheim, Vingolf, Breidablik, and Valhalla. Gladsheim is the place where the gods hold their court. Breidablik is home to the gods, Baldur, and his wife, Nanna. Vingolf is where the goddesses and their children are located. It is here that the goddess Freya holds her court for those who visit her. Valhalla is the home of fallen heroes and is said to be located to the west of Asgard. It appears as a beautiful palace in which nothing is impossible. Every wish is fulfilled, and nothing goes wrong, thus making it an extremely desirable place to live. However, this perfection comes at a cost since the only way anyone can enter Valhalla is by dying in battle. Here, the dead warriors reside and train for the upcoming battles of Ragnarok.

Vanaheim

Vanaheim is home to the Vanir clan of gods, who are thought to be opposites of the Aesir. It is located in the western region and is said to be a land filled with fertility, prosperity, and beauty. Not much is known about the Vanir family of gods except that they are peaceful people who hold wisdom in high regard. It is understood that Asgard and Vanaheim exist side by side, and while they are different, they share a similar bond of kinship and friendship.

Alfheim

Alfheim is the realm of the elves and is said to be located between Asgard and Midgard. It's a beautiful world where all life is present, from trees, flowers, and animals to other kinds of creatures such as birds, insects, fish, and mammals. It's a place where the elves can live among these creations while they practice their own form of magic. Many of these creatures are said to be magical in nature and embody different aspects of the elves' magic, such as fertility, rainfall, and even death. Like Midgard, this realm is also home to many gods who, for the most part, remain neutral in all conflicts. They only intervene when their human followers need help or protection due to the constant threat Helheim poses to them. Their realm is also known for being where peace, sympathy, and love reign.

Midgard

Midgard is the world of man and is located in the center of the Nine Worlds. It's a beautiful world filled with majestic wonders, beautiful creatures, fields, forests, water, mountains, valleys, hills, and even underground caves. It is also where many gods reside when they are not in their own realms, acting as protectors of the humans who dwell there. For this reason, it's a frequent target for the forces of chaos since they want to destroy everything that exists in this world due to its relationship with the gods of order. This realm is also believed to be surrounded by a serpent called Jormungandr, which is so large that its body circles the entire world to the point where it eats its own tail. A prophecy says that at Ragnarok, Jormungandr will rise from beneath the ocean, flooding the land and poisoning its inhabitants.

Niflheim

Niflheim is the realm of darkness where even gods fear to tread. It's a barren, frozen wasteland filled with ice, fog, and clouds that are said to drift from one world to another through Yggdrasil. In this desolate land is the ice-cold spring of Hvergelmir, where all waters flow from. Hvergelmir is thought to be the source of all waters in the Nine Worlds, and its waters are seen as being poisonous to any who would drink them.

Another feature of Niflheim is a bridge that connects Asgard to this realm but is guarded by massive wolves. Should a person attempt to cross the bridge, they risk falling into the chasm of Niflheim and being killed before they even get there. The gods are often said to cross this bridge to travel through Yggdrasil, but attempts at invasion or crossing this bridge are rarely successful.

The only way for someone from Asgard to survive Niflheim and its inhabitants would be if they were already dead. Their world is also home to a massive dragon named Nidhogg, who sits at the bottom of its deepest chasm and gnaws away at one of Yggdrasil's roots. It is said that Nidhogg will continue this process until the day comes when it finally chews through the root, which would result in Yggdrasil falling and all Nine Worlds being destroyed.

Nidavellir

Nidavellir is a stony, mountainous plane that is said to be located beneath Asgard. Its inhabitants are dwarfs, also called dark elves. They are said to be able to make anything imaginable with their magical hammers and anvils, which they forged themselves. The objects they craft are said to be indestructible by any means, including the most powerful forces of chaos that exist in the Nine Worlds. Nidavellir is also the only world where time runs differently than it does in the other eight planes. In some stories, time is said to move much faster in Nidavellir than in other worlds. It is explained that while only seconds pass in Nidavellir, many more years have passed in the other Nine Worlds.

Jotunheim

Jotunheim is the place of the giants and another plane that exists beneath Asgard to the east. It's similar in nature to Nidavellir in that it's a rocky place, but instead of being inhabited by powerful dark elves, it's home to giants known as Jotuns. Jotunheim is also said to be filled with giant mountains, valleys, and caverns littered with ice and snow. This realm is known for producing the most significant natural disasters, such as earthquakes, volcanoes, and floods. It's also a place that is fertile for the formation of the darkest magic, black fire, and earth magic, which is the source of the Jotuns' raw, untamed strength.

Muspelheim

Muspelheim is the realm of fire and is believed to be located south of Midgard. It is too hot for anyone to survive except for the fire giants. They live in a realm that's as rocky and barren as it is hot, scalding, and fierce. This world is said to be filled with lava rivers that cascade down into hot pools of magma, volcanic rock pits that spew up a liquid fire, and infernal flames that burn with such intensity the very fabric of the Nine Worlds burns before them. It's also the realm where Surtr reigns as king and is only concerned with one thing, which is the destruction of everything.

Helheim

Helheim is the realm of death and is a dark, dismal place where those who die are doomed to remain forever. The only exception is those who die in battle on the side of either order or chaos since they have the right to enter Valhalla instead. Apart from this, those who die without being killed in battle are doomed to roam Helheim forever. It's a place where the air is said to be cold and frosty while the environment is filled with nothing but mist, fog, and clouds.

The only sound that can be heard in Helheim is the wind blowing through the dead's bones while they wander its frozen plains. The land appears barren, with no sign of life except for a lone house called Utmo, which serves as one of the nine gates leading into Valhalla. Utmo is located deep within Helheim's inaccessible mountains, and its doors are buried within a massive block of ice that has never been melted.

Shamanic Journey through the Nine Realms

As mentioned earlier, a shaman possesses the ability to journey through the realms to communicate with the gods and other supernatural entities. Shamans have practiced this ritual since the dawn of time, which is why some cultures practicing it today consider it to be part of their ancestral shamanic tradition. This journey works through trance, a specific state of consciousness in which the spirit can communicate with those residing on the other side. The ability to enter a trance is often brought about by using specific hallucinogenic plants, drumming, dance, or all of the above.

To perform a shamanic journey through the realms, a shaman must first pick the realm they wish to explore. The most commonly visited realms are Asgard, Nidavellir, and Jotunheim; however, some would like to go to Muspelheim, Hel, or Alfheim. The reason why a shaman would do this is that they usually have a special purpose there. Some go looking for answers, others intend to deliver gifts to the gods, and others go in search of allies who can help them in the fight against chaos.

Regardless of why they are traveling there, a shamanic journey through the realms is a long and arduous task that often takes months, sometimes years, of preparation for the shaman. They will have to go through several stages before entering a trance and visiting the Nine Worlds. The journey's first stage is called "Eir Self," where the body and soul are cleansed of any impurities. This is done by fasting for several days and going through purifying rituals. This is followed by lengthy meditation where the shaman will keep their body in a magically induced state of trance for days at a time.

During this stage, the shaman's body is completely numb and will feel very light, like they are floating above themselves. In this state, the shaman will often hear voices and see visions. They will also experience various sensations like heat, coldness, touch, and pain. If a shaman can pass this stage, they will be ready to travel through the realms. Though entering a trance seems easy to some, those who undergo this discipline often complain of how painful it can sometimes be.

Once the shaman has mastered the art of entering and leaving the trance at will, they are ready to enter the great shamanic journey. This ritual is usually performed at night when the veil between this world and the other is at its thinnest and most vulnerable. This journey works as a kind of supernatural smokescreen that creates an imaginary tunnel between the realms. All the shaman has to do is follow the tunnel to the other side.

Chapter Three: Norse Deities to Guide You

The Norse pantheon is organized into three main factions; the Aesir, Vanir, and Jotnar. Each of the three factions has its own culture and pantheon of deities. The Aesir are the gods of battle, the Vanir are the fertility gods, and the Jotnar are those closely tied to nature. Let's get to know each of them and see how they relate and interact with one another and the practice of shamanism.

The Aesir Clan

The Aesir are the gods of battle and poetry, law and society, art and wisdom. They are the protectors of humanity, and it is their job to make sure that the forces of darkness do not break into Midgard and overthrow or kill the inhabitants. They are the main focus of Norse mythology, the gods most often mentioned in stories and myths. Despite this, they are by no means omnipotent. They often have to work together to achieve things and rely on more than just their powers and skills to overcome obstacles. The Aesir seem to have been based on the Germanic war gods or a Germanic ideal of the perfect human. They are quite similar to humans but have a better grasp on their own abilities and are stronger and wiser than humans. There are twelve main gods in the Aesir clan, as well as scores of other lesser deities and demigods. The ones most related to Shamanic practices are:

Odin

The ruler of the Aesir and the god of wisdom, among other things, Odin isn't just one of the most well-known deities. He is perhaps the most important. He is called Alfadir (All-Father) for his many roles as the father of gods and men. He is a god of many names, roles, and aspects. Some people will say he isn't a god of war when he is. Others will say he isn't a god of wisdom when he is. The truth is that Odin is both and neither of these things. He gives battle his thoughts, creative mind, and unique perspective. In Odin, you'll find a god complicated to understand and impossible to completely define by any single set of human values.

As the ruler of Asgard, Odin is rightfully the leader of the Aesir, and he is a wise leader. He decides what actions the Aesir will take and follows through on them with great precision and his famous spear, Gungnir. There is no action to be taken by the divine that he does not consider first and weigh carefully. He's not a reckless man, as some would have you believe. He does have an occasional tendency toward overconfidence, although it's usually justified. He will often make rash decisions in favor of his desire for knowledge and understanding without considering potential negative results or other options. He also has a tendency to act on his own sometimes, even in the face of the advice of his wiser and more experienced wife, Frigg.

Odin is often called upon for assistance by practitioners of Norse shamanism. His ravens Huginn and Muninn (thought and memory) fly over the world, gathering information for him. His power of seiðr draws on his ability to access knowledge from many sources simultaneously; some people call this scrying or telepathy. He is also a master of the runes, possessing his own called Odin's rune or the wyrd rune. There is no deity more associated with shamanism than Odin. He has his outbursts of temper, his moments of wisdom, his moments of doubt, and his moments of surety.

His symbol is the triskelion, representing the world's interconnectivity. His color is red, the color of action and power. His animal is the raven, and his creatures are the wolves. To gain favor with the All-father, learn as much as you can, and don't be afraid to try new things or even fail at them a few times. Changing yourself is the most valuable gift you can give him, and you'll be rewarded with greater knowledge, insight, and the power to overcome even the direst of situations.

Heimdall

Heimdall is the guardian of the gods. His job is to sit at the border of Asgard and guard the Bifrost, a rainbow bridge that leads to other realms. Heimdall is also a god of prophecy and divination who has great knowledge of worldly and otherworldly things, but he is also known for being rather vain, pompous, and showy. His greatest attribute is his sense of hearing, making him a valuable asset in knowing what's happening in the world around you. This allows him to act as a bridge between different worlds, to hear the messages coming through the ethers and act on them. He can also tell if you are present in a place where you are not supposed to be or if someone is using his name out of ignorance. He can tune into the rhythms of life that resonate with him and give you the clarity you need to know where your path lies.

Heimdall reminds us that we are all interconnected and interdependent upon one another. He shows us that it is okay for us to seek knowledge from unexpected sources and that we should always look for ways to cross boundaries, build bridges between people and understand our place in this world. His color is golden yellow, representing the sun's rays and warming properties. His symbol is a horn or trumpet, which he uses to sound the call to battle in Asgard and to warn the Aesir of danger coming from Jotunheim. Chrysanthemum is a flower most associated with him, which embodies his sense of beauty and artistry.

Heimdall's favor can be gained by communing with nature, paying attention to all the sounds around us, and using these sounds to enhance our awareness. A great way to call upon him is through singing a song, as it contains rhythm and a certain power that can be very transformative and healing. If he accepts to connect with you, he will often send you a message about something you may have forgotten or that you need to remember.

Frigg

The wife and consort of Odin, Frigg, is the goddess of motherhood, marriage, and wisdom. She is a gentle, beautiful goddess who has great compassion, warmth, and power. She also has a fierce temper and never hesitates to defend her loved ones when necessary. Like her husband, she is brilliant and is especially honored by the Aesir for being with them through the years that have genuinely tested their loyalty.

Frigg is often a central figure in ancient Norse healing practices. Her power can often be seen in the health and well-being of those who seek her love and aid. Her appearance on a shamanic journey brings gifts of knowledge, strength, and courage that can help you overcome many obstacles on your path toward health or recovery. Her role in the world of shamanism is closely tied to her role as a mother. She is the one you turn to for help when you find yourself in need.

Her assistance can be a boon to almost any type of healing, from physical illness to emotional problems and even severe trauma. Her color is blue, symbolizing her wisdom and her ability to see things as they are. Her flower is lavender, whose scent causes clarity of thought and increased senses. Her sacred symbol is a distaff, which is the tool used by Norse women to spin yarn for clothing, art, and magical practice. You can gain her favor by taking care of family and loved ones. She will often reward you with clearer insights into situations and relationships that concern you.

Thor

Thor is a god of iron and thunder. He symbolizes the wild energy that brings strength to our lives and makes us strong enough to overcome life's challenges. Some people may think of him as an angry or violent god—that is not the case. However, he does get angry or overly enthusiastic from time to time in his pursuit of a worthy goal.

Thor is the embodiment of the passionate warrior in us all. He is a god who encouraged us to fight for what we believe in, especially when we are faced with great adversity. He helps us find our own strength and power. He is a deity of action and can be trusted to help us overcome whatever stands against us. Whether that is physical, spiritual, or psychological obstacles, he will help you prevail. Even if he doesn't, his actions will inspire courage and strength based on his own example from what he has faced before.

It's said that Thor is actually a shape-shifter himself. His ability to take on many forms gives him power over wild animals and those who wish to harm Aesir Gods, including giants and trolls. It is important to note that while he is a god of thunder and protection, Thor does not seek out problems but solves them when they arise. He is sometimes called upon when a shaman needs physical strength or courage to overcome something in their life. His energy is often sought by martial artists and those who have made a career of fighting in the military or law enforcement. He will give you the courage and will to fight for your goals and values, which can be very important in all walks of life.

Thor's symbol is a hammer, Mjölnir. It represents strength and honor – alongside lightning and protection. This god is mostly associated with the color red and has several red animal forms, including the bull and the boar. To gain favor with him, you could pay homage to him with a bowl of red berries or perhaps a red flower from the North.

Loki

Loki is the god of mischief. He manipulates and deceives fate, often with devastating consequences for both gods and men. He is a trickster, doing harm either for no reason at all or to teach a lesson to someone who deserves it—but sometimes, he just does things out of spiteful curiosity. Even when he doesn't mean harm, not only does the victim of his mischief suffer from his actions, but he is also often punished as well.

Loki's main attribute is intelligence, which he uses to create mischief and dishonesty whenever it suits him. He is a god of doubt and distrust who, at the same time, is a great seeker of knowledge. He never stops learning and is always ready to learn from teachers, books, or nature itself. He likes to be seen as an enabler for change that brings wisdom and knowledge to those who would otherwise have remained ignorant.

Some people turn to Loki when they are sick of the complacency of their lives and want to shake things up. He can help you discover some deceptions that you may have lived with for a long time and never noticed. He can also help you change your life for the better, sometimes in ways that are so disruptive that it comes as quite a shock, but it is always worth it. His symbol is the snake or dragon; if he accepts you to connect with him, he will often send you a message through your dreams.

He is usually symbolized by the color orange or yellow, the colors of fire. It represents the change in our lives that can be brought about by our own actions or the actions of those around us. Loki's favor can be gained through listening to nature and the wisdom that comes with it, becoming involved with art or craft, or learning to look at things with a fresh perspective so that inspiration can be found and all potential is discovered.

The Vanir Clan

The Vanir are a family of gods and goddesses who live in Vanaheim. Where the Aesir are attributed to war and society, the Vanir are connected to the natural world, each representing a particular aspect of it. They are the guardians of mankind's interaction with nature. They are a community of gods who are closely related to each other and also to the Aesir. They are known for their wisdom, magic, and passion in all aspects of their lives. They are nurturers who bring peace and prosperity to the people and to the territory they inhabit. They are also known as the bringers of fertility and plentiful harvests.

The Vanir are a reminder that all of nature is sacred, including death itself, because nature is life and death to those who know it well enough to see its beauty. They represent nature in its rawest form, where magic exists and dreams come true, where death is not an end but a beginning to life. Their wisdom and magic are very real –

and meant to inspire those who seek their help to develop their own powers. They are the great shamans of the Norse Gods, and they teach the magic of life and the elements.

Freyja

Freyja is the goddess associated with love, fertility, women, and beauty. She is also the goddess of understanding and foresight. Often depicted in her chariot pulled by two felines, she helps us communicate with the universe and other realms through inspiration and guidance. She teaches that love and beauty give us permission and the power to overcome anything. As the goddess of sensuality, ecstasy, pleasure, and lust, she embodies the joy of physical passion and intimacy, the intense sexual drive between men and women, and those between a person and nature or a person and their inner self.

In addition to helping with love, fertility, and beauty issues, Freyja is also a seasoned volva, capable of great wisdom that only comes from an understanding of the interconnectedness of all life and the importance of living in harmony with nature. She is a keeper of ancient knowledge, which flows through her to us, whether in dreams or waking visions. She can help us to communicate with the spirits who guide us when we don't know what to do or help us overcome obstacles, especially when those obstacles are related to our personal growth and development.

Her experience with seidr magic gives her the wisdom to know what is possible and what is not and to use that knowledge as a tool for our own empowerment. She helps us to understand the power of creativity, art, and self-expression. As the keeper of the veil between the worlds, she helps us see things from new perspectives to choose which path will best suit our needs. Her symbol is the heart-shaped pendant or necklace, representing our capacity for love and passion in all aspects of life. You can offer her a piece of jewelry to express your creativity to gain her favor. She has links to the color red, which is associated with passion, love, and lust.

Freyr

Freyr is the twin brother of Freyja and the god of fertility, prosperity, and peace. He is the god of the sun and of summer, hence his association with wealth, good harvests, and plenty. He gives us the gift of life and rebirth. His symbols are the boar and the phallus. He is a benevolent god who provides comfort in times of need.

Freyr may also be called upon to help you to recognize and change negative patterns in your life. He is well acquainted with the negative aspects of human nature and can help you overcome them – or at least recognize how they affect your relationships with others. Like his twin sister, he has great empathy for those who feel misunderstood or mistreated. His magic is very compassionate and gentle but strong and effective. To give favor from the god of fertility, you can offer him a fig, which represents abundance and fertility. He has links to the color yellow, which is associated with the sun.

Njord

Njord is the god of the sea and seafaring men. He is considered to be the parent of Freyr and Freyja, with whom he shares dominion. He is the god of wealth, farming, and the sea. He is known for his magic and is skilled at channeling energies into others. Like many Norse gods, he is considered very wise and knows much about magical arts and natural medicine.

To the shaman, Njord embodies the mysteries of the deep, especially those hidden below the sea, which connect to wisdom, magical power, and the greater spiritual realms. He is closely connected to the elements of earth and water and can help you with issues related to the sea or seafaring. He is also known for his ability to communicate with animals. His magic can be very effective at helping you to understand your spirit guide and how to work alongside your spirit animal.

Njord's symbol is the seahorse, and his color is green. He may be called upon for assistance to find life answers and gain clarity about your true path. He can also help you to overcome issues with wealth or prosperity. He'd appreciate a nugget of gold as an offering of thanks for his help.

The Jotun Clan

The giants, known as the Jotnar or Jotun, are not exactly gods but are very powerful in their own right. They are the spirits of what we would consider the "natives" or "originals." They can be described as the embodiments of nature and, as a result, have a completely different outlook on life than that of the Aesir gods. They are not interested in agriculture or commerce and only want to live in harmony with nature, unconcerned with human affairs.

They are known for having tremendous magical power, which is tapped into by those who practice seidr and shamanic sorcery. Many are considered to be shape-shifters and masters of illusion and enchantment. Their magic is very insidious and difficult to control. However, if you work with them, you may have the opportunity to learn more about yourself and your dreams and the different aspects of life on this planet. They teach us the value of compassion and tolerance, especially towards those who appear to be different or less favored by the gods.

Ymir

Ymir was the first being to emerge into being, and he emerged from Ginnungagap, the great void from which all things were born. He is the ancestor of all life and was considered to be the first to experience death. His blood fathered all of the giants, and his body became the foundation of the world. Ymir is thus thought of as being the anti-archetype for everything in our world, especially human beings. He represents nature at its purest.

He can be called upon to help you connect with the deepest realms of nature, which is widely considered to be the source of all life and inspiration. Those who wish to ascend into the realms of the Jotnar must grasp the principles of nature because they will call upon Ymir's wisdom in their own form of magic. He can also be called upon to assist with guardian work and protector spirits. He is considered to be a great shamanic tie to the realms of death, where all things begin and end.

Sutr

Sutr is the Jotnar who rules over the depths of Muspelheim. He is a god of darkness who reigns over the hot subterranean realms that lie deep within Yggdrasil. He is a powerful and dangerous god whose magic is focused on control of the mind. He is the god of destruction, rebirth, and renewal and is associated with volcanic activity.

Sutr represents not only the destructive qualities of fire but also that ancient part of yourself that allows you to follow your intuition. He is a god of primal instincts and can help you to break down old patterns of behavior that no longer serve you. He craves life force, and those who call upon him find themselves facing challenges that will forge new strength within them. Like all Jotun clan members, Sutr represents nature's raw power and is thus a god of chaos and unpredictability.

Once you have connected with the powerful forces of nature yourself, calling upon them in their own forms to serve your will is incredibly easy. It doesn't matter what form they take for you; it's simply a matter of recognition. When we allow the powers that surround us to guide our actions and direct our destinies, we give them direct access to our energy. Thus, we liberate ourselves from illusions about who we are and how we may be able to do things.

When we communicate with the forces of nature, we are actually making a connection to the divine in the most primal sense. By speaking with them, we gain perspective on our relationship with reality rather than simply the narrow perception we are accustomed to. This better understanding can be used for our own benefit and for the good of others. Deities often represent certain forces or principles which are universally important to us. It doesn't matter if you subscribe to a monotheistic or polytheistic worldview. When you're communicating with these forces, you're directly connecting to the divine.

If you choose to call upon the Aesir or Vanir gods for help and guidance, you are communicating with those beings directly interested in the maintenance of order and the continuing existence of life. These include Thor, Odin, Freyja, and others who embody and defend the principles of skillfully preserved tradition and nobility. By calling upon these gods, you are also asking for their assistance to maintain order in your own psyche as well.

If you choose to connect with the Jotun clan, you'll begin a conversation with nature itself. These beings are not connected to spirituality but are directly connected to the forces of nature on Earth. They are powerful beings who are capable of being truly benevolent toward humans. When you communicate with these gods, you are allowing yourself to reconnect with the forces of life and existence. This can re-connect you with your place in the universe and help you realize your true potential.

What really separates the gods from humans is the ability to exist in a form that is not necessarily bound by our physical rules of reality. They can see and experience the world freely, and this freedom allows them to be much more powerful than we could ever imagine. We can connect with them by opening ourselves up to new experiences and allowing ourselves to transcend where we are now. With enough willpower, we can reach beyond our limitations and rise above our perceived shortcomings.

Chapter Four: The Norse Medicine Wheel

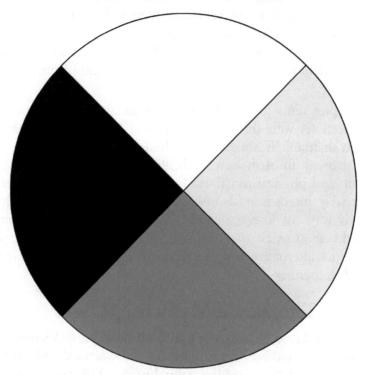

Norse medicine wheel.

Every culture has its traditions and rituals surrounding health, healing, and medicine. This tradition is known as the Sacred Hoop or the Medicine Wheel for shamans. It is a unique medicine wheel that is depicted as consisting of four directions that surround a central point. It is known for being a healing and transformative tool and has been used by most cultures in one form or another. In this chapter, we will talk about the Viking Medicine wheel, which is slightly different from that of other cultures because they take their gods into consideration when creating the wheel and its directions.

The Norse Medicine wheel is important because it places humans in a perspective where they recognize each direction as having specific traits. For example, the East is where the sun rises, a time of renewal and rebirth. West is where the sun sets, a time of introspection, and the North is a direction of strength, endurance, stability, and resourcefulness. The different directions are also known for their relationships with certain deities. For example, Thor is linked to the East; Odin is linked to the North. This can become very important in healing because, like in other cultures, each direction represents certain pieces of information and traits that are often required in a healing ritual. It is a way to consider the symbolism of the gods when healing and manipulating the natural elements.

This chapter aims to describe the four main directions and discuss their connections with the Norse gods and how this may have been involved in shamanic healing rituals. The four directions can be used to guide a shaman through several healing rituals, such as divination, meditation, and physical practices. In our culture, we sometimes forget these everyday interactions between ourselves and nature. By learning about their ways of interacting with nature, we can learn from their insight and begin to view our own methods in a new way, perhaps even learning about alternative ways to heal ourselves through intuition and the natural elements.

The Norse Medicine Wheel

The Viking Medicine Wheel is a tool both Norse and Viking shamans incorporate. It is a pictorial representation of the actions and interactions between humans, deities, and the natural world. This allows for a better understanding of one's connection with nature and the deities that can be summoned at any time, including when performing shamanic healing rituals. The Wheel is divided into four quadrants and eight directions. The central point is what connects all the quadrants together and can represent several things. In some instances, it is seen as the Earth, while in others, it is seen as the Earth and Asgard combined. This can be important to consider while performing healing rites because it shows that a shaman must be able to bridge the gap between his earthly and spiritual worlds.

The directions are clearly marked by cardinal points, i.e., North, East, South, and West, which also include mythology and folklore that has been passed down throughout time. Each direction is linked with a specific deity, which makes the directions more recognizable to the Norse and Viking people, and each one holds certain symbols that carry its own importance, as we will now see

The North Direction

The North is known for being the direction of raw energy and formless potential. It is linked to the All-father, Odin, who can be seen as the guardian of that direction. This direction is known for being a place of wisdom, insight, magic, and divination and is said to contain both positive and negative elements in terms of magic. Odin is believed to have hung himself from Yggdrasil to learn the knowledge of the runes, the ultimate sacrifice of himself. With this single act, he transcended all limitations of humanity, a transformation that resulted in him becoming boundless unadulterated energy, much like the one in the North.

Without Odin's protection, venturing into this area of shamanic experience would be very dangerous and could result in unintended consequences. Odin's strength allows him to personify the wild and untamed energies of the North while still remaining in control of these forces. One can gain passage into this unknown and mystical dimension through his strength.

The North-East Direction

The North-East direction is linked to the god of war, Tyr. In Norse mythology, Tyr lost his arm during a fight with the monstrous wolf Fenrir, which has an interesting symbolic meaning for his connection to this direction. Tyr represents a protective mentality, not necessarily war, but a firm mentality that is not afraid of conflict or confrontation. It is seen as a safe and warm place to go, but there is always a certain amount of danger present.

Tyr represents the ability to remain calm in any situation and take over in times of need. The North-East direction represents perseverance and determination while still being able to be accommodating, as well as being able to use these qualities when necessary. It is also linked with the ability for adaptability. Fenrir represents our base desires and primal instincts, a part of us that can be controlled or harnessed when we need to but can be unleashed if we cannot control it.

As the guardian of this direction, Tyr can take charge of these instincts and channel them into protecting the safety of its users or - in necessary situations - assist in protecting the world. The North-East is also linked with a certain type of aggression in the form of combat and fighting. Tyr cannot be conquered by those approaching him, for he is an unstoppable force, a guardian of all things good and just.

The East Direction

The East direction represents balance, a neutral area where neither good nor bad can enter. It is believed that all things in the East direction can be used for good or for evil, for it is a place of neutrality. It represents an open mind to the possibilities and opportunities that surround us. The East direction is not considered a particularly magical direction because it does not hold any real energy or power but rather simply serves as a medium for everything else. It also represents self-reflection and the practice of religion and spirituality alone.

This direction has been compared to being like an empty canvas; whatever you make of it will be created by yourself, and its purity cannot be tainted by others no matter how hard they try. Thor, the god of thunder, guards this direction. Thor is the ruler of the mind, and the mind is a direct reflection of the soul. He guards the East because that is also the realm of the giants, who can be interpreted to represent our ego, a constant threat to the soul. Thor's representation of the mind is used to maintain a balance between our inner and outer world and ourselves and others. Through Thor, we can become more aware of our own minds. He can help control our wilder desires, which plays a significant role in self-reflection and spirituality.

The South-East Direction

The southeast direction is linked to Freyja, the goddess of fertility and love. She is seen as a goddess of the senses and pleasure. Her ability to bring joy and pleasure into the world is unmatched, and she is linked with passion and sex. She is also seen as an example of female power, something prevalent in Norse culture, and she rules over all things that can be counted, bringing order and balance to life.

The South-East direction represents sensuality, sexuality, purposefulness, fertility, and prosperity, thus giving it a significant relationship with humans in developing the mind and body into maturity. Freyja reminds us to enjoy the pleasures in life, to experience joy and love, as well as to follow through and make our dreams a reality. She also represents creative coordination and the ability to combine things into one harmonious whole.

The South Direction

The South can be associated with Baldur, the son of Odin. This direction deals with action and is associated with the ability to take control. It is linked with the concept of being grounded, as well as being able to make decisions based on logic and reason. The South direction also has a link with the universe, having its place in the cycle of life and death. Quite often, in mythology, this direction represents death and rebirth. It is linked with mortality, pathology, and disease. It represents the soul's incarnation into the physical body and the possible subsequent release of this soul back into the cosmos. Baldur's death in mythology is representative of the death of youth and innocence, the cyclical nature of life, and the inevitability of death. It is seen as a direction of awareness, intelligence, and understanding, a place beyond the "veil of illusion," where one can see the true nature of things.

The South-West Direction

The South-West direction deals with the concept of the subconscious mind and is related to Hel, goddess of the underworld. The underworld is the realm of the subconscious mind and is associated with all things hidden. It contains the realm of dreams where we can relive our past and experience our fears. The subconscious mind is also related to deception, illusion, and temptation.

Another aspect of this direction is the balance of forces between the universe and the physical world, as represented by the two sides of Hel's mirror. The South-West direction represents introspection. It encourages us to think about our lives and reflect on what we are doing in this lifetime. This can represent bringing a tragedy or hidden issue into the light or coming to terms with a loss or grief. It can also represent something that has been repressed but still remains buried deep within the psyche, something that cannot be ignored or escaped from, no matter how hard you try.

The West Direction

The West is associated with Njord, the sea god. It deals with necessary limitations and barriers, as well as the need for boundaries. It is linked with the concept of being grounded and having a clear mind, able to make decisions on a logical and rational basis. It is a place where you can find inner truths and access the instinctual mind that gives us the ability to understand nature. It deals with past actions, wrongdoing, or things done in the past that must be paid for – or the process of healing after such wrongdoings. It is linked with a balanced soul, which deals with the knowledge and wisdom that comes from experience and from within.

The West also has a close relationship to the concept of time, also having a place in the cycle of life and death. It is a direction of acceptance and positive change. Njord, who is also Saturn, the god of time, encourages us to face reality and accept it as it is. He is a god of inner growth who points out where we are being held back and what we must do to move forward. The West represents the balance between experience, familiarity, and cosmic order.

The North-West Direction

This direction has direct links to the god, Freyr. It is the realm of the elves, the beings of enlightenment and the agents of positive change. It is linked with inner knowledge, wisdom, and understanding. It is where we can get in touch with our "higher" or intuitive self or the origin of our souls.

The North-West direction represents the universe and the source of all things. Freyr can help us tap into the universal energies and bring them into our lives to help us grow and develop into fullness. It is linked with spiritual transformation and the transmigration of souls. It ties in with healing, regeneration, love, and fertility. This direction also has a close relationship with sexuality and spiritual abundance, both essential for growth on any level.

How Did the Ancients Use the Medicine Wheel?

The Norsemen were some of the most powerful and feared people on Earth, yet they were peaceful farmers. Like all of us, they craved a healthy and fulfilling life. To create this, they used the medicine wheel to guide their spiritual and physical growth.

They believed each direction was a realm with its own spirit, which could influence the human soul. Through mystical ceremonies, they used the direction's god to gain higher awareness or help to heal or make changes in their lives. They believed that nature had a rhythm that could be felt in the four seasons and four directions. This wheel represented the cycle of life and death and the balance between the physical world, the soul, and the universe. They understood that each direction had positive and negative attributes and learned how to find their place amidst these opposites.

The Medicine Wheel and Modern Shamanism

The Norse were advanced and intelligent people. Perhaps they knew things we have forgotten that can help us live a more fulfilling life. The concept of the medicine wheel and its use has been around for centuries, and it is a good model of how to live and experience a happy, balanced existence. Using the direction gods as guides, this ancient Norse practice can provide us with valuable insights into our lives. Just as the direction spirits can teach us about ourselves through their stories, so too can we learn valuable lessons by looking at where we are in our lives right now in relation to these gods.

It is believed that this practice can help us understand the concept of "balance." Balance is one of the most important things in life, whether it applies to our physical, mental, or spiritual state. Perhaps it is best seen as the "flow and ebb" of life, and the ancient Norse saw this concept as an essential part of their lives. Even if you do not believe in the direction of deities, you can still use this practice to get a glimpse into how you are living your life at this very moment and how you can improve your situation.

The concepts found within the Norse Medicine Wheel are as relevant today as they were thousands of years ago. They can be used by anyone from all cultures, religions, or backgrounds, and they can be used in a variety of ways, like during meditation, card readings, or other divination practices. As with any divination tool, the information it gives us is not necessarily a complete picture of how we should live our lives. It can only give us an insight into where we are and what we can do next to improve our situation. The point of the medicine wheel is to give you a starting point, but it may be up to you to decide what action you take from here.

Chapter Five: Sacred Herbs and Plants

Meditation, magic, and alchemy are just a few of the many ways humans have attempted to gain knowledge about the universe and use nature's power for their own benefit. Shamans were the first healers who sought to understand the world around them and use it as a power source. They studied nature and used what they learned to guide people through difficult times.

The plants that shamans sought out were extraordinary in many ways. Some were better for quick relief from pain or to treat diseases, while others were better for spiritual enhancement and trance induction. This chapter will take you through these different kinds of plants and explain what they can do for those seeking natural wisdom or who wish to connect with the divine powers of nature beyond just physics.

Angelica

Angelica plants were used to kill pests in ancient Greece and Rome.
https://pixabay.com/images/id-1594701/

Angelica (*Angelica archangelica*) is a perennial plant with one of the strongest smells of all plants. The plant can grow up to six feet tall and produces white-to-pink flowers in the summer. The Greeks and Romans used the plant to kill rats, vermin, and other pests. It has a variety of uses and medicinal properties, including antibacterial, anti-fungal, analgesic (painkillers), antioxidant, diuretic (lowers blood pressure), appetite stimulant, demulcent (soothing), emmenagogue (promotes menstrual flow), expectorant (aids in the removal of phlegm) antihistamine and anti-ulcerative.

- Magical Properties: Angelica strengthens the power of other herbs and their effectiveness when used in mixtures. It is said to protect against psychic attacks or to be an aid when you are trying to raise the power of your spell work. Angelica increases milk production in nursing mothers and is also said to be an antidote for poisonous mushrooms.

- How to Use: Some people like drinking tea made with angelica root, and others like using tinctures made with the herb. To make a tea, simply add a small amount of angelica to a cup of boiling water and steep for three to five minutes. If you do not wish to drink tea, add the leaves to a bath and soak in this for five minutes.

- Affirmation: I choose wisely, live in harmony, and work harmoniously with the elements of nature for my benefit and for the benefit of those around me.

Ashwagandha

Ashwagandha.

Ashwagandha (*Withania somnifera*) is a perennial herb belonging to the family of Solanaceae. It is often used as Ayurvedic medicine, so you may see it referred to as Indian ginseng. It has a rich history and many uses worldwide, including being recognized as a sacred herb in Indian culture. The plant has been used for centuries by Ayurvedic practitioners and has been used in rituals and ceremonies for healing, longevity, strength, and more. It is used to lower blood sugar in diabetics and is also an effective anti-inflammatory. Studies have shown that ashwagandha can help those with Alzheimer's, cancer, and HIV/AIDS.

- **Magical Properties:** Ashwagandha is believed to be a protective herb that wards off evil and attracts good luck.

- **How to Use:** You can make tea by boiling ashwagandha leaves with a few lobelia leaves until they become dark green and aromatic. It is also widely used in incense blends.

- **Affirmation:** I am open to the flow of life and am connected to the earth's magic, which brings happiness and prosperity into my life.

Bay Leaves

Bay leaves.
https://pixabay.com/images/id-272961/

Bay leaves (*Laurus nobilis*) are like tiny evergreen trees on the end of a branch. The leaves are dried and used in cooking. They are effective stimulants that can increase mental alertness and improve your memory. Bay leaves are also an effective antiseptic and can be used to clean cuts, insect bites or stings, fungal infections, and other skin ailments. They contain tannins, which help to prevent infections and can also help to reduce symptoms in chronic itchy skin conditions such as eczema, psoriasis, and hives. The chemical constituents in the leaves can also be used to treat asthma.

- **Magical Properties:** Bay leaves are used in divination, making them a good complimentary herb for those who are not used to using herbs or who have a fear of using them. It is said that bay leaves have the power to attract good luck and fortune while warding off evil spirits.

- **How to Use:** To make incense, burn dried bay leaves on an incense burner and scatter the smoke around your home to create a spiritual atmosphere. You may also use bay leaves in spell work to attract luck and money regularly.

- **Affirmation:** I am protected by the power of nature, love, and the divine feminine force of creative energy.

Bergamot Mint

Bergamot mint.

Photo by David J. Stang, CC BY-SA 4.0 <https://creativecommons.org/licenses/by-sa/4.0>, via Wikimedia Commons: https://commons.wikimedia.org/wiki/File:Mentha_aquatica_Citrata_0zz.jpg

Bergamot (*Mentha citrata*) is a mint-family herb that is known for its distinct citrus aroma. It has a long history of use in aromatherapy and as an antiseptic. Bergamot yields a high concentration of limonene, which has disinfectant, antibacterial, anti-viral, and anti-fungal properties. It can also be used to reduce fever and help those experiencing symptoms associated with the common cold. It is also used to treat acne while increasing the production of bile, which helps with weight regulation.

- **Magical Properties:** Bergamot is a sacred herb and has historically been used in witchcraft and magic, such as banishing and binding spells. It aids in communication with spirits and guides or protects you as you move through life's journey. In some traditions, it is used to appease the gods by burning a smudged bergamot stick during an incantation or spell.

- **How to Use:** Bergamot is most commonly used in incense and is burned as an offering to the gods. It can also be added to a bath or used to rinse your face of toxins before bed. It can be added to bath oils and used to take a bath after meditation or ritual.

- **Affirmation:** I choose the path of my dreams and visualize my success with creativity, kindness, and attention to detail.

Chamomile

Chamomile.
https://pixabay.com/images/id-3489847/

Chamomile (*Matricaria recutita*) is a perennial herb that is also sometimes called English chamomile. It belongs to the Asteraceae family, which is at the top of the daisy family. Traditionally, it has been used as an anti-inflammatory and to treat aches and pains like headaches or muscular pains. It also has mild sedative and antiseptic properties. Chamomile is believed to be useful for those who suffer from skin conditions such as eczema, psoriasis, and acne. It is an effective anti-allergenic, helping the body to heal while preventing allergic reactions or immune system overreactions.

- **Magical Properties:** It is a good tea to use when you are seeking inner peace, and it is also used in spells and rituals for love, healing, and divination.

- **How to Use:** Chamomile can be used as incense or added to a bath to aid relaxation. It can also be infused with a massage oil or added to your shampoo.

- **Affirmation:** I am protected by the power of the divine feminine, and there is no evil in me or around me.

Cowslip

Chamomile.
https://pixabay.com/images/id-4968515/

Cowslip (*Primula veris*) is an herbaceous perennial plant of the primrose family. It is also known as a fairy cup and has long been used as a medicinal herb. It can be used to reduce fevers and treat symptoms like mild infections and inflammation or skin conditions such as eczema or psoriasis. Cowslip contains both antibiotic and anti-inflammatory properties that help to soothe allergies, inflammatory bowel disease, and ulcerative colitis. It is also a diuretic, which helps flush toxic wastes out of the body.

- **Magical Properties:** As Freyja's herb, cowslip has long been used in spells and rituals for love, healing, and divination.

- **How to Use:** You can make an infusion by steeping the flowers of the cowslip in warm water. Use this to rinse your face and clear your skin of toxins. You can also use it to make tea or add it to a bath.

- **Affirmation:** I create the life I desire and acknowledge my divine connection with the earth.

Cumin

Cumin.

Cumin (*Cuminum cyminum*) is a flowering plant in the family of Apiaceae. It is a common ingredient in many cuisines worldwide, particularly in Indian, Middle Eastern, and Asian dishes. Cumin has many healing properties that date back to ancient times. It has anti-inflammatory and anti-diabetic properties and qualities that can help fight cancer and prevent heart disease. Cumin also aids weight loss by supporting blood sugar levels and reducing the absorption of carbohydrates.

- **Magical Properties:** Cumin evokes protection and security from evil spirits or someone trying to cast a spell on you. It is most commonly associated with Heimdall and can be used to help you manifest your desires into the physical world.

- **How to Use:** Cumin is often added to food to flavor it and disguise its strong taste. It can be added to teas, soups, and stews. It can also be used as a natural perfume oil or added to herbal baths for purification purposes.

- **Affirmation:** I am fully supported by the Earth's creative energy, which carries me through my journey with grace and ease.

Dill

Dill.
https://pixabay.com/images/id-8104/

Dill (*Anethum graveolens*) is a flowering plant belonging to the family Apiaceae. It is an essential herb in many cuisines across the world, popular as a food flavoring or spice. Dill has antibacterial, anti-viral, and anti-fungal properties. It can be used to make an effective herbal mouthwash to maintain healthy teeth and support digestion and general cleansing. It can also aid weight loss by supporting weight management.

- **Magical Properties:** Dill is often used in spells and incantations that work with divination or change one's current situation by drawing a new path to follow.

- **How to Use:** Dill can be made into a cold compress, used in a bath, or added to a herbal infusion

- **Affirmation:** I can evaluate my life without judgment and find the best path for my dreams, intentions, and goals.

Elm

Elm.
https://pixabay.com/images/id-316360/

Elm (*Ulmus alata*) is a large deciduous tree belonging to the Ulmaceae family. It is an iconic species that play a vital role in stabilizing and maintaining the health of the ecosystems in which it grows. Elm has anti-microbial, anti-viral, and anti-fungal properties. It can be used to treat yeast and fungal infections like athlete's foot while relieving inflammation associated with these conditions and reducing pain. Elm is also used within the food industry to produce alcohol, vinegar, and more.

- **Magical Properties:** The elm is a sacred tree associated with the forces of nature in many cultures. It symbolizes balance, magic, and healing while representing spirit guides and protection. Elm has been historically used in spells to protect against witchcraft or negative energies and invoke self-love. Elm wood can be carved into an ornament or totem to connect with spirit guides and is often associated with Odin.

- **How to Use:** Elm bark can be used in a bath, as a tea, or added to herbal infusions.

- **Affirmation:** I can find a balance between my internal and external worlds and cultivate an environment that nurtures the evolution of all that exists.

Fennel

Fennel.
https://pixabay.com/images/id-2617/

Fennel (*Foeniculum vulgare*) is a perennial herb that is also occasionally used as an ornamental plant. It is a member of the Apiaceae family, commonly grown as a vegetable and consumed as a salad herb. Fennel has long been used in herbal medicine to treat health conditions like diarrhea or other stomach upsets, bloating, and gas. It can also help relieve symptoms of menopause, such as hot flashes, while fighting breast cancer by preventing the spread of cancer cells.

- **Magical Properties**: Fennel is commonly used in spells to promote happiness, abundance, and fertility.

- **How to Use:** Fennel can be added to a bath to promote relaxation and purification.

- **Affirmation:** I am blessed with good health, prosperity, and well-being which will continue throughout my life.

Fly Agaric

Fly agaric.
https://commons.wikimedia.org/wiki/File:AD2009Sep20_Amanita_muscaria_02.jpg

Fly Agaric (*Amanita muscaria*) is a large reddish-orange to yellow mushroom with white spots or patches on the cap. They are members of the Amanitaceae family and contain psychoactive substances, especially ibotenic acid and muscimol. Fly agaric typically grows in birch forests in summer and autumn. This fungus is not considered edible due to its toxicity but has been used as an entheogen by various cultures since ancient times. The mushroom was used by indigenous Siberians in the past, who believed it had the power to reveal the locations of hidden treasures or healers.

- **Magical Properties**: Fly agaric is often associated with nature spirits and deities such as the Norns and Mimir, who watch over the hidden realms. It represents healing, growth, and transformation while providing protection from disease and storms. Fly agaric also has associations with time travel and astral projection, which makes it ideal for astral travel rituals.

- **How to Use:** Fly agaric can be made into a cordial or added to food or drinks

- **Affirmation:** I honor the gifts of nature and allow my consciousness to merge with the universe for me to experience its beauty and transformations.

Garlic

Garlic.
https://pixabay.com/images/id-1238337/

Garlic (*Allium sativum*) is a species in the onion genus "Allium." It is sometimes known as "poor man's treacle" since it has long been used to treat infections and illnesses. Garlic has anti-cancer and anti-microbial properties. It can also help reduce stroke risk and prevent blood clots leading to heart attack or stroke. Garlic also helps to lower high cholesterol levels.

- **Magical Properties:** It is commonly associated with Thor, who would often request a garland of garlic during cleansing ceremonies. The herb is used to promote psychic abilities and increase overall vitality. It is also used to promote clear thinking and strengthen the will.

- **How to Use:** Garlic is boiled in vinegar, and then the liquid is strained. A small amount of this liquid is then rubbed on the temples to invoke visions. It can also be added to a bath or infused into a massage oil or natural perfume oil.

- **Affirmation:** I move forward from the past into my future with grace and ease, freely exploring and discovering the magic of life.

Hawthorn

Hawthorn.
https://pixabay.com/images/id-4024488/

Hawthorn (*Crataegus monogyna*) is a member of the Rose Family, often used as a medicine or herbal supplement. It has been used to treat anemia (low red blood cell count), heart issues, and even cancer. Hawthorn is used in the traditional medicine of many countries, including China, Japan, and India, as an anti-inflammatory and antibacterial herb.

- **Magical Properties:** Hawthorn is most commonly used in spells to increase knowledge, wisdom, and clarity of thought.

- **How to Use:** Hawthorn can be eaten raw, added to a herbal infusion, or made into a tincture. Hawthorn flowers can also be used in making garlands for prayer and meditation. They are dried and then woven into wreaths hung over doorways or windows as an offering to spirits or placed on altars as symbols of honor.

- **Affirmation:** I can easily focus my thoughts and bring them into reality through the power of my intention.

Henbane

Henbane.
https://pixabay.com/images/id-2306579/

Henbane (*Hyoscyamus niger*) is a flowering plant in the same family as nightshade. Henbane contains deliriant alkaloids, including hyoscyamine, which produces a similar effect to belladonna and atropine. Henbane has been historically used as an analgesic and muscle relaxant, especially during childbirth. The Vikings devised a way to convert this otherwise toxic herb into a rather intense stimulant that granted them an edge during battle.

- **Magical Properties:** Henbane has powerful magical properties. It is often used in spells to communicate with and learn from spirits, manipulate time and space, increase intuition and psychic abilities, and enhance magical prowess.

- **How to Use:** It can be made into a cup of tea, added to a herbal infusion or tincture, or smoked.

- **Affirmation:** I bring love and inner peace into my life by trusting in the process of my journey and the wisdom of the universe.

Mugwort

Mugwort.
https://pixabay.com/images/id-1338208/

Mugwort (*Artemisia vulgaris*) is a perennial herb used to treat inflammation and pain. It relieves an upset stomach from nausea and may also help to alleviate tension headaches or regulate menstruation. Mugwort invokes calmness, clear thinking, and devotion in spell work or meditation. It has also been used to treat depression, epilepsy, and as a sedative for insomnia in some cultures.

- **Magical Properties:** Mugwort is associated with the spirits of the dead who can communicate with the living. It is commonly used to summon spirit guides and communicate with ancestors. It is also used when engaging in divination practices and enhancing dreams.

- **How to Use:** Mugwort can be added to a bath, placed under the bed, or used in an infusion. It can also be turned into incense and burned during ritual practices.

- **Affirmation:** I find meaning within all of my experiences.

Mistletoe

Mistletoe.
https://pixabay.com/images/id-16393/

Mistletoe is a parasitic plant that grows on trees. It is used in herbal medicine to treat heart conditions and boost the immune system. The herb has anti-viral properties that may help prevent colds, flu, and other infections while reducing inflammation, treating hypertension, and preventing hemorrhages.

- **Magical Properties:** Mistletoe has been used in Germany since the thirteenth century as protection against witchcraft. It promotes greater awareness and sensitivity to the needs of others while also amassing information. It is also used in spells to enhance psychic powers by connecting the mind and spirit and increasing intuition.

- **How to Use:** Mistletoe can be eaten or drunk as tea. It can also be added to a bath, made into a tincture, or placed on an altar for protection from the evil eye.

- **Affirmation:** I am calm and centered in my life, bringing guidance to all that I encounter.

Nettle

Nettle.
https://pixabay.com/images/id-474351/

Nettle (*Urtica dioica*) is a common plant used for hundreds of years as medicine or spice. It is high in fiber and includes vitamins A, C, and K and many trace minerals like iron, manganese, and zinc. Nettle is often used to treat anemia because of its high iron content. It is also known to treat erectile dysfunction and even improve hair growth.

- **Magical Properties**: Traditionally, nettle has been used in protection spells due to its association with the element of water. It is used to banish negative energy or entities from the home while at the same time protecting against outside forces.

- **How to Use:** Nettle can be made into a tea or burned as incense to clear negative energy, negative thoughts, and bad vibes.

- **Affirmation:** I can let go of worry, fear, and negativity while embracing the abundance of my life.

Viper's Bugloss

Viper's bugloss.

Viper's Bugloss (*Echium vulgare)* is a perennial biennial herb with yellow flowers. It is known to treat muscle spasms and pain while also lowering blood pressure. Viper's Bugloss contains saponins, steroid-like chemicals that may slow the growth of cancerous tumors. It is associated with vitality and strength, as it can help improve memory and protect the body against ill health.

- **Magical Properties:** Viper's Bugloss is known to foster a trusting and helpful nature, making obtaining information from spirits and divine guides easier. It is also used in spells aimed at inspiring one's creativity or creating a connection between oneself and the natural world.

- **How to Use:** Viper's Bugloss can be eaten raw, dried, and added to a herbal infusion or made into a tincture.

- **Affirmation:** I can listen and observe, allowing myself to become more connected with the natural world around me.

Watercress

Watercress.

Watercress (*Nasturtium Officinalis*) is an annual herb that is related to the mustard family. The plant is a powerful diuretic that may help prevent or treat cancer. It may even increase the production of certain hormones that stimulate human growth cycles.

- **Magical Properties:** Watercress is used in spells that help one tap into the wisdom of their own subconscious mind and communicate with spirits from other realms. It can be used to help you interpret your dreams and is often added to a mixture of other herbs when making dream pillows.

- **How to Use:** Watercress can be added to a salad, eaten raw, or made into tea.

- **Affirmation:** I can communicate clearly with my loved ones on the other side, helping me achieve personal growth and understanding.

Chapter Six: Growing a Shamanic Mind

The shaman is a master of trance. During the shamanic state of consciousness, spirits communicate with - or visit - the shaman. Often, this type of trance lasts for only a few moments, but it has been scientifically proven that such experiences can cause profound changes in brain function and neurobiology, as well as new connections between existing neuronal networks.

At its most basic level, falling into a trance state is about dissociation from oneself. The person enters an altered space-time continuum which enables them to not always be aware of their body or surroundings when they are visiting other realms (or dimensions). In other words, the person's body takes a backseat to their consciousness.

What Is the Shamanic State of Consciousness?

The shamanic state of consciousness can be described - and experienced - by those fluent in this altered reality's language. Due to our Western cultural context, few people have ever experienced it, and because most of us are wired to operate at a very different frequency to the shamanic state, we often feel dazed or dizzy when we enter a similar altered state. As a result, many shamans still struggle to explain what they do and how they do it, even though it is the very heart of their practice.

Generally, the shamanic state of consciousness is a way of existing or being that differs from our everyday experience. When we experience something through our senses (seeing, hearing, touching, smelling, and tasting), it is generally considered to be a solely physical event. Within that context, most people do not believe that a spiritual realm exists, and thus those things we experience via this realm are generally considered to be imaginary or make-believe.

However, shamans have been shown (by science) to have neurological and neurobiological differences from non-shamans, and all shamans know intuitively that this is so. In many ways, the shamanic state of consciousness is a mind-body synchronization that produces a kind of "super consciousness." This experience is only possible for those who have developed a deep level of awareness and sensitivity to the subtle energies that permeate the physical world. Because this awareness enables one to tune into and interact with the subtle realms, shamans are believed to be able to observe events in these other realms that we cannot see in the physical realm.

In his book "Shamans Through Time," anthropologist Michael Harner compared the shamanic state of consciousness to dreaming: "*The dreaming state is a unique and highly developed form of consciousness in which the dreamer experiences worlds that are completely alien to waking reality.*" Once you realize that any dream is representative of a mental process taking place within your mind while you are asleep and not a literal experience involving other realms or entities, it becomes easier to understand how various aspects of the dream are representative of psychological and emotional issues lying underneath your conscious awareness.

Harner succinctly explains the process of dreaming, stating that the dreamer is conscious while their body sleeps but that what they are experiencing is not happening in their physical world. They are "consciously unconscious." He further explains that a lucid dreamer experiences a wholly other space where they can interact with beings and events in this other realm, which has its own set of rules and logic. The lucid dreamer is conscious enough to remember the details of their experience upon waking up (or straying back into this realm) and have some control over what happens during the experience, like how to alter this new reality and how to interact with related beings and events.

However, the shaman has a totally different relationship with this realm. They are only partially conscious while in this trance state. This trance state is not a space where their consciousness is altered but where they are still fully conscious within their physical body and may be consciously aware of their surroundings in both the physical and other realms simultaneously (or transcendentally). It is here that they go to experience and learn about other worlds and dimensions and also travel through time and space to experience different situations firsthand. The shaman is no longer unconscious but rather is fully conscious while "deadened" in this trance state.

The Shamanic Trance

A shamanic trance begins in an altered or "just noticeable" state of consciousness. If you were to see a shaman in such an altered state, they would appear to be daydreaming or merely in a quiet state where they are thinking deeply. This is the beginning of the shift into shamanic states of consciousness. It becomes visible through various micro-movements and gestures. A person will begin breathing quickly, perhaps rocking slightly from side to side, and becoming partially aware of their environment. Being aware of their surroundings is the first step toward entering a trance.

Very Light Trance: Once in a trance, heart rate, blood pressure, and brain waves slow down significantly. The person enters what is known as a very light trance, which is where the person becomes very light in body and mind but not entirely out of it. A person may also enter a very light trance while awake or actively engaged in some sort of activity. In such cases, the physical movements are more exaggerated, and the person may create some sort of movement that is not part of whatever activity they are engaged in. For example, when a person is absent-mindedly waving a pen around in their hand as they speak, that could indicate that they are entering a light trance state.

Light Trance: The next trance stage can look like deep sleep. The person will be lying down, their eyes will be closed, and their body posture may be somewhat stiff or rigid. The physical appearance of this stage will vary greatly from one shaman to another because it depends on how each shaman was taught to enter this type of trance state and what specific goal they have while doing so.

Medium Trance: Medium trance is characterized by the person making movements or sounds typically associated with non-ordinary realities. This is the point at which a person's body will be in a relaxed state, and their hands will begin to move in a way that does not correspond to normal motor skills. It could be described as similar to semi-automatic writing, with the difference being that a person in a medium trance may also vocalize sounds, whereas semi-automatic writing does not include vocalizing.

Deep Trance: Deep trance is when physical movement and vocalization become partly involuntary. The person will look like they are asleep but could also make sudden jerking movements. They may also flop slightly from side to side while they are speaking.

Very Deep Trance: A very deep trance is when the person is fully out of their body and has no body awareness whatsoever. In a very deep trance, the person may perform actions that are uncommon for them or that do not correspond with how they usually act. For example, a very deep trance state could result in a person attempting to fly, walk over water, or speak to people not in the room.

Shamanic practitioners often use very deep trance states to call upon other shamans and spiritual beings. During this state, a person may see visions or technologically augmented or even artificial-intelligence-based visions of other realms and beings in those realms. These visions may come from anywhere throughout the universe, and they can be perceived through different senses: acoustic, visual, olfactory, tactile, and even taste. At other times, a person in such a deep trance state will speak out loud to landscapes they perceive or to ancestors and other spiritual beings that only they can perceive. The following are common traits of the hypnotic state:

- A sense of tranquility and feelings without emotional content.

- Automatic obedience to suggestion (suggestibility).

- A feeling of detachment from the body and, sometimes, from the real world. The body may feel light, heavy, or numb. Sometimes one can be aware of some stimuli in one's environment but not others, sometimes unaware of all stimuli, and sometimes everything seems unreal. The experience is highly subjective and individual.

- A lack of self-control over behavior and feelings. One can act in ways that are otherwise not understood by oneself. One may give the appearance of being in a daze, asleep or unconscious.

- A feeling indicating, at times, an increase in mental activity and intellectual function, sometimes accompanied by a sense of enhanced perception. Often there is also a feeling of ineffability. This can be experienced as an enhanced ability to believe things that would have been impossible before (wishful thinking). It can also induce the feeling that one is "on drugs" or "high."

Scientifically Proven Brain Changes that Occur during Shamanic Trance

Multiple documented brain studies have shown that during shamanic trance states, the electrical activity in people's brains changes significantly. These changes occur in the areas of:

1. **The thalamus,** where electrical communication between various regions of the brain is controlled. The thalamus is responsible for filtering the messages relayed between different parts of the brain and relaying them to their appropriate parts, controlling part or even all of a person's movement, sleep, or consciousness.

2. **The cortex,** where all perceptions are processed. It also controls awareness and thought. This part of the brain is responsible for perception and higher functions such as abstract thinking and planning. A person may perceive things that would not normally be perceived (hallucinations) in this area during shamanic trance states.

3. **The amygdala,** where emotions are processed. The amygdala is responsible for our biological reactions to fear and other types of emotions. During a shamanic trance, the electrical activity in this part of the brain decreases significantly.

4. **The hippocampus** is responsible for general memory formation and mental processing. The two hippocampi analyze the information they receive and freely relay it to the cortex to be processed. During shamanic trance states, electrical activity in this area greatly increases, allowing for enhanced memory functions that go beyond normal limits.

Other research done on receptors in the brain supports these findings. There are multiple kinds of receptors in the brain, including receptors that bind with chemical neurotransmitters, those that bind with oxygen, and those that act as pathways for electrical signals. Neurotransmitters are chemicals in the brain neurons (nerve cells) released when impulses pass through them. These neurotransmitters then bind to various receptors and trigger a response. The transmission of messages between neurons is thought to occur partly by altering the frequency at which certain neurons fire (or activate).

Now let's focus on two neurotransmitters; noradrenaline and acetylcholine. Acetylcholine is generally involved in memory, learning, and attention. Noradrenaline has many functions, including being involved in the brain's response to stressful situations. It is thought that altered levels of acetylcholine and noradrenaline could account for some differences between ordinary states of consciousness and trance states.

In this study, researchers found a decreased amount of acetylcholine receptors in the cortex but an increased amount of receptors on neurons in other areas during trance states. This could help explain why people under these conditions may be more susceptible to hallucinations and altered perceptions than they would normally be. This study also found that the number of noradrenaline receptors increased in certain areas, explaining the jumpy and anxious feelings sometimes associated with this altered state.

For those who take part in shamanic drumming, there's a significant reduction of the stress hormone cortisol. It's been suggested that the lower amounts of cortisol may be related to the heightened psychological functioning reported during trance states. This means that shamanic drumming can produce brain changes and stress-relieving physical effects.

How shamans achieve altered states of consciousness is not well understood but is usually attributed to their mastery of the use of the entheogens that induce these effects. Shamans say that spirits power these drugs and that their ability to enlist these spirits for help in healing and accessing knowledge is solely due to their purity and lack of ego. However, entheogens are also available in forms that are toxic or poisonous, and these are often used for malevolent purposes. The use of entheogens for spiritual purposes is exclusively a human phenomenon.

In many cases, the spirit takes possession of the shaman's body and speaks through it. The spirit may take over the shaman's voice in such a case, producing unusual sounds or words. Shamans may also have visions while they hallucinate. Shamans undergo extensive training before letting a spirit enter their bodies, so they can handle a spirit's presence without going insane or losing their minds completely. One way to quantify a shaman's strength is his ability to handle spirits.

Utiseta Meditation

The Utiseta meditation is a form of mindful repetition of the act of breathing when inhaling and releasing when exhaling. It is performed in a sitting position, with the individual's attention focused on the process of inhalation and exhalation. Once the individual's attention is focused on their breath, they can focus on the sensations inside and outside themselves. Shamans usually use it when they go into an altered state of consciousness. This practice has been a part of traditional shamanic cultures – such as the Amazon and Peruvian shamans who use it to access their spirits. It is believed to be an essential technique for a shaman, and this proves true in many cases. In fact, some practitioners have observed that shamans use techniques of the Utiseta meditation during certain stages of a trance state to deepen and intensify the experience or even bring shamanic experiences under their control.

For the Norseman, Utiseta meditation was a sacred practice in which he would enter an altered state of consciousness and communicate with his ancestors. It was a type of ritual prayer in which the Norseman would focus on the act of breathing while meditating on the spirit of his ancestors. In this way, the Viking could bring himself into a state of awareness that enabled him to communicate with spirits and perform seidr. The Norseman believed that the spirit of his ancestor was able to communicate with him through these types of rituals.

This meditation is not the only way shamans believe they can access their transpersonal experiences, but it is still an effective and powerful one. The ability to enter into this state of consciousness allows shamans to have access to a wealth of information and be in contact with spirits and other beings. They can also use this state of consciousness to heal by communicating with their ancestors or even other shamans for aid or guidance. This form is considered very sacred, and its power is great, which accounts for the fact that it is still practiced today.

Benefits of the Utiseta Meditation

Utiseta meditation has been proven to reduce stress and improve serotonin levels. It has also been proven to strengthen immune systems, increase the ability of individuals to deal with pain, and allow a person to be more open-minded in their thinking. This is because it is a type of exercise in conscious breathing and only requires an individual to focus on the act of breathing. This form of meditation allows shamans to be more aware of their bodies and what they feel during states of altered consciousness. It helps them to learn how to control the state of their consciousness and does not cloud their mind with any type of psychological interruption. This form of meditation is a great way for shamans to access the information they need to heal their patients and is also used by them to help people achieve higher states of consciousness.

Shamans believe that breath is the starting point of all life, and they speak extensively about "breath" when they are attempting to teach their apprentices the ways of shamanism. They believe that breath contains all life forms, and as it circulates through one's body, different types of information are sent through it. They believe that breath contains a great deal of information about one's health and emotional state. They recognize that a well-timed breath can give them a feeling of strength and power, making it an ideal technique for shamans who are looking to enhance their ability to heal others in their communities.

Shamans have often been credited with controlling their minds in ways most normal people cannot, but what is not commonly known is that the mind and body are connected through the power of breath. The question is not whether shamans can control their minds but rather control their breath and, in turn, the mind.

How to Perform an Utiseta Meditation

Utiseta meditation is a very simple exercise that can be performed in several ways. To perform this exercise, you must set aside at least 20 minutes per day for practice. As a beginning, you may decide to perform the meditation for 5 – 10 minutes per day and gradually increase your time limit as you become more comfortable with the exercise. You'll also want to make sure that you are in a quiet and comfortable place where no one will disturb you while performing this exercise. One of the most important things to remember is that it is important not to force oneself into entering into a trance state for Utiseta meditation to be effective. If you are serious about learning shamanism and using this type of meditation to help facilitate your learning, then you must approach it from a place of curiosity and respect.

Step One: You'll want to sit in a comfortable and upright position on a cushion or chair that is large enough to support your legs and back.

Step Two: You'll want to close your eyes and focus on your breath as you slowly inhale and exhale. It is important not to force your breathing by making it faster or slower than usual, but rather let the breath move at its own pace. Take several minutes for this step until you feel relaxed and comfortable.

Step Three: To begin the meditation, you'll want to focus on breathing in for a slow count of four. Once you have reached four, hold that breath for a slow count of eight before exhaling slowly for a count of eight. This is one cycle when doing the Utiseta meditation.

Step Four: After exhaling, you'll want to pause for a moment before inhaling again. You need to repeat this process several times to create a form of breathing that is steady and even.

This is an example of how you can begin the Utiseta meditation, but there are different ways to perform it. If at any time during your practice you feel yourself losing focus or becoming distracted, then you must stop for a moment and focus on the breath as it enters and exits your body until you regain your composure and are ready to start again.

Improving Your Results

Many people get frustrated when they attempt this type of meditation and are unable to achieve an altered state of consciousness. This is normal, as it takes time and practice to reach a relaxed state of body and mind. You'll need to allow yourself plenty of time to adjust your breathing to be balanced and slow. If you have problems with this technique, many other techniques have been proven to help increase a person's ability to achieve the shamanic state of consciousness. These include:

Mantra: Mantras are words of power that have been passed down from generation to generation and are actually believed to contain a certain amount of energy. When spoken out loud or repeated to yourself in your head, mantras allow a person to focus on a sound and create the type of vibration that can be used for healing. Shamans believe that a person can use the power of these mantras to tap into different states of consciousness.

Visualization: Visualization is a technique that uses the mind's eye to help guide oneself through different states of consciousness. Shamans believe that one can reach a much deeper state of consciousness when using visualization as opposed to breathing exercises, as they require the use of an individual's imagination. Visualization is an excellent way for shamans to access the information they need to help in their healing endeavors and assist individuals in attaining a higher state of consciousness.

Primal Rhythms: Primal rhythms are techniques that date back to ancient times and are believed to have been used for many generations. They include things such as dancing, drumming, chanting, and using a rattle to create a rhythmical sound. Shamans can maintain their focus and balance by rhythmically connecting with their mind, body, and spirit. It is an excellent way for beginners to enter into a higher state of consciousness while exploring shamanism.

Sacred Plants: The use of various herbs that have been dried, smoked, or ingested is a common practice for shamans to use in their rituals and healing ceremonies. Herbs like ayahuasca, fly agaric, and peyote are known to help a person tap into their subconscious mind and help them to achieve an altered state of consciousness. These herbs are often used in conjunction with other shamanic practices to fully appreciate the benefits they can provide.

While it is important to remember that Utiseta meditation is not the only way for a shaman to achieve altered states of consciousness, it is still considered one of the best and most effective ways for anyone interested in shamanism to enter into a trance state to begin their journey. As a person who is interested in learning shamanism, you must understand that many techniques exist and learn to focus on what feels right to you. Utiseta meditation may not be for everyone, but it can help open up a door that leads to an entirely new way of thinking and a deeper understanding of the person you are.

Chapter Seven: Connect to Your Ancestors

Ancestral connection is an umbrella term that captures the various relationships we can have with our ancestors. These relationships can be biological, spiritual, or a mixture of both. The gifts and attributes of these ancestors can range from supportive and empowering to challenging. Realizing that ancestral connection can benefit us in many ways is vital for any shaman engaged in a shamanic journey.

Ancestral connection involves a wide range of topics. These include our ancestors' history, lifestyle, habits, and death rates. It also includes their ancestral relationships, such as their offspring, grandchildren, and siblings. Our ancestors can be from our own bloodline or other bloodlines that we are connected to by way of marriage or adoption. These ancestors can be people we have known personally in life or those who are only known through research and study.

By connecting to ancestors, we get to know them better and better understand our own lives by learning more about their lives. This understanding will greatly help us as we connect with the land and learn the lessons our ancestors lived by. We can also take strength from the fact that many of our ancestors were able to survive and thrive despite their circumstances.

Ancestral connection is important for any shaman because it teaches them about their origins, culture, and traditions. This will help them gain a greater understanding of why they are who they are, as well as why they do what they do. Understanding why we do things in the ways we do allows us to make sense of our lives. This, in turn, helps us cope with present life conditions more positively, especially when dealing with any negative situations or emotions such as anger, resentment, jealousy, or isolation.

The ancestral connection also provides us with a spiritual support system. This is particularly important for shamanic journeyers because it gives us a chance to have an ally in the afterlife. Ancestors cannot only watch over us, but they can also help us in various ways during the journey by providing information, guidance, or even direct assistance. The ability of our ancestors to watch over us enables them to protect our health and well-being. They can do this by helping to ward off negative energies and spirits that may try to cause harm or injury when we are vulnerable in the dream or trance state. This is particularly helpful when we are traveling in the lower or upper worlds, where there are very powerful forces present that can do us harm.

Connecting with our ancestors can also provide us with the opportunity to ask them to help us heal. We may ask them for their assistance in healing physical and psychological issues. We might request that they help protect us from negative influences such as spirits, entities, and forces of nature. Sometimes we may even ask them to help remove harmful thought patterns or habits from our astral body that prevent us from being our best selves.

Perhaps the most important gift that ancestral connection brings is wisdom and knowledge. The more we connect with people who came before us, the more we learn about life and ourselves. The experiences and knowledge of our ancestors give us an awareness that connects us to their wisdom. This, in turn, helps us learn how to make sense of our lives in a way greater than the sum of its parts. By learning how our ancestral experiences shaped who we are, we can use this wisdom as a guide to help us make sense of what it means to accept ourselves and be the best versions of ourselves.

Ancestors in Ancient Norse Shamanism

Like other cultures, ancient Norse culture regarded ancestors as a source of guidance, wisdom, and source of power. Shamans used the spirits of dead ancestors to help them in the process of discovering their own powers, learning how to interpret dreams, and developing shamanic techniques. While the spirits were primarily needed to help with practical things such as healing or protecting people from danger during their travels in trance states, their influence could also be seen in shamanic quests. The ghosts of shamans' dead ancestors would often appear to them in visions and dreams, providing necessary assistance or guidance for personal or spiritual growth.

Ancient Norse shamans used different names to refer to their dead ancestors. Most of them were referred to using the word *alfer* or *alver*, which is the term for ancestors in Old Norse and some Scandinavian languages. These spirits could appear either as a single entity with one name or appear in groups as various individuals with various names. The appearance of these spirits would depend on the purpose of the shamanic experience and usually took the form of human-like beings dressed in typical Norse clothing. However, they could also be seen as half-human, half-animal creatures or other shape-shifters like dragons or foxes. The spirits of the dead ancestors would often wear a ring on their left hand, helping them to appear in human form, but they also could turn completely invisible and appear as balls of light or clouds to guide the shaman.

The relationship between the shaman and their ancestors wasn't always healthy. The dead can be just as cruel and impulsive as they are wise. There is a saying in Norse society that goes, *"An ancestor is to be feared most by the one who brings dishonor or shame."* In ancient Nordic societies, the dead were always honored and appreciated, but they were also feared. Ancestors could be either benevolent or malicious, helping you in your journey or trying to make it more difficult. While they did provide help, they also represented a great threat to anyone who violated their rules. Potential threats from ancestors came in three forms – violation of taboos, neglect of ancestors, and disrespect. Shamans who made avoidable mistakes in their work, who were lazy and didn't give their all to the people they were supposed to protect (or violated their own taboos or rules), had reason to fear their ancestors. The ancestors would often slip into their children's dreams and scare them in various ways, mostly as a means of helping them understand the gravity of their actions so that they could change and improve themselves. It was believed that if you fell sick, it was likely because your ancestors were angry with you. If your mind can't stop thinking about something or someone, it is likely because they are trying to influence your thoughts, and so on. One of the reasons these spirits interfere with their descendants is to help them learn something new or overcome a problem. For shamans, this could be anything from finding lost items to understanding complex spiritual concepts or solving everyday problems.

Choosing an Ancestor to Connect With

The best way to connect with your ancestors is to pick a specific ancestor with whom you feel a strong connection and a strong desire to connect. Pick someone who you feel has had a large impact on your life or someone who has played an important role in the areas of life that you want to work on. Talk about what kind of connection you have felt with this person and why. The most important thing for the relationship is respecting each other and sharing life experiences. It is important to develop an understanding of who this person was and what their life meant to them. The closer your relationship with your ancestor, the stronger the bond will be, so dedicate yourself to learning everything you can about them and their experiences.

In Norse Shamanism, it is important to have a good relationship with the spirits of your ancestors, but it is equally important to make sure that the relationship is reciprocal. You need to make sure you give back as much as you take from them. This could be anything from paying tribute with offerings and libations to rituals of thanks or prayers to helping the community in some way. A good rule of thumb for most cultures is to give things that the ancestors would appreciate. This could be gifts of food, clothes, or other items they may have cherished. The idea is to help these spirits reconnect with you and help them see that they have an important role in your life. Honoring your ancestors will help you connect and communicate with them and help you grow as a person, and establish your own relationship with this part of yourself.

Connecting With Your Ancestors

There are many methods of connecting with ancestors, depending on your beliefs, desires, and personal preferences. The most common practices are:

1. **Writing a Letter.** This is a very simple and straightforward way to reconnect with your ancestors. Just sit down and write a personal letter to the spirit of the deceased ancestor. In this letter, talk about how much they have affected your life and how you feel

close to them. The letter's content should be as personal as possible, but ensure that you are respectful and honest. After you have written the letter, leave it somewhere they may find it or burn it as a way to release its energy.

2. **Visiting the Grave.** This is a very common practice in most cultures all around the world. The most important thing to remember when visiting a grave is respect. Never visit an ancestor's grave on a whim or behave disrespectfully while visiting their resting place. The purpose of this visit should be to reconnect with your ancestors and learn more about them as individual people, not simply dwell on their death or become angry at them for leaving you behind. Take some time to think about who your ancestor was and how they were connected with the things you value in life. Think about what they may have liked, what they may have wanted, and why. It is important to remember that ancestors are not dead, only transitioned to another plane of existence. They are still very much alive, watching over you and helping you.

3. **Smudging.** Smudging is a simple but effective way to connect to ancestors and other spiritual beings. It consists of burning a bundle of sacred herbs, usually sage. This bundle is lit and spiraled around yourself in various directions (usually clockwise) as you visualize an energetic cleansing wave. While doing this, you can chant specific prayers or sing specific songs. Once you have finished smudging, sit down, and visualize the ancestors before you. Invite them to your space and let them know you acknowledge and appreciate them.

4. **Going on a Shamanic Journey.** You can perform a journey to connect with your ancestor, but most often, you'll be looking for guidance or information about a specific subject. A journey is an ideal way to achieve this goal because it puts you in an altered state of consciousness, giving you a direct line to your ancestors and other spirits of the cosmos.

5. **Rituals.** These are a powerful way of connecting with your ancestors, but they can be very complex and specific to certain cultures. In Norse Shamanism, several rituals could be used for working with ancestors, depending on the circumstances. One common ritual was the blot – an offering of an animal sacrifice to

the spirits, usually in honor of your ancestors or other important spirits in your life. Many variations of the blot were practiced, but they all had the same goal in mind – to release energy and send it to other spirits.

6. **Building an Altar.** The creation of an altar is a wonderful way to connect with your ancestors. Altars are dedicated to specific spirits and can be made to honor those who have passed or to connect with the spirits you are currently trying to bond with. An altar can be as simple or complex as you want, but it most often consists of photos, items of value, offerings, and other things that link you to the spirit in question.

7. **Meditation.** This was a very common way that allowed ancient cultures to connect with their ancestors and spirits. Meditation can be used to aid communication between the living and the dead, for guidance, and for a myriad of other purposes. A good way to start is by meditating every night before bed. Simply sit still in a comfortable position and focus on your breath. Focus on nothing but yourself, your breath, and the silence that surrounds you for about ten minutes. After about five or ten minutes, you'll start to notice your mind wandering and thoughts popping into your head. This is completely normal in the beginning. When these thoughts arise, simply acknowledge them, acknowledge where they came from, and let them go, returning to your breath. After a few minutes, your mind will start to quiet down, and you'll become at one with your breath again. Meditation is the perfect way to connect with the spiritual world around you and your ancestors.

8. **Shamanic Drumming.** This is a very powerful way to connect with ancestors and make peace with them. The shamanic drum is a unique sacred instrument that can open spiritual communication between people. It is believed that your heartbeat will mirror the sounds created by the drum, giving it the power to connect with ancestors or other spirits.

9. **Animal Communication.** The shamanic connection with animals is a very important aspect of shamanism. Animals are very different from humans because they communicate on a level the human mind cannot comprehend. Animals communicate with each other through the sense of vibration. In the same way,

shamans connect with spirits and ancestors by feeling their vibrations. This practice can be used to commune with ancestors for their wisdom, guidance, and healing purposes. To perform animal communication, you have to focus on the animal itself. You can do this by looking at a picture or an article pertaining to this specific animal, but it is recommended that you seek a live specimen. Look into the eyes of the animal and try to feel its energy. Do not think about anything else, and do not allow your mind to wander. Simply connect with the animal until you can feel its vibration inside yourself. This is how animals communicate with each other and how your ancestors can communicate with you through them.

10. **Visualization.** Visualization is a very powerful way to reconnect with your ancestors. To visualize them, close your eyes and relax. Once you are relaxed and ready, visualize the ancestor you wish to connect with (the spirit's appearance is up to you). This could be a physical manifestation or just an impression of their energetic presence. If you have trouble visualizing the ancestor, imagine that you are in a time machine, transporting yourself into a specific time and place where the ancestor was living. Where they were, what they were doing, and any other details you can think of will help you visualize the ancestor better. Visualizing your ancestor in this way will create a connection between both of you and allow the spirit to be aware of you.

While it may seem as if we are really closed off from our ancestors, this is far from the truth. They are with us all the time, helping us and guiding us on our paths. Acknowledging their presence in your life is important for your growth and happiness. There are many ways to achieve this recognition, but the most important thing is for you to do it with respect and honor for yourself and equally for your ancestors.

Chapter Eight: Fylgja, Your Spirit Guide

The idea of a guide or companion who is linked to a person's destiny and fortune can be seen in many cultures, with the concept having its roots in Shamanism. The hunter-gatherer people of North America attribute this to animal totems, while the Ancient Greek gods were sometimes seen as guides or companions. In both cases, these entities are considered supernatural beings that are not human and have the power to either help or harm those seeking them out.

In Norse culture and myth, it was called the fylgja. The fylgja is responsible when people believe they are connected to a spirit that guides them. Fylgja can be interpreted as a supernatural being or a spirit linked to the destiny and fortune of an individual – and who acts as their companion. This is not something you can see or touch, but it is there for those who believe in it.

The Fylgja and the Shaman

The fylgja is the personal spirit guide of individual people, but to the Norse, it is also a manifestation of the guardian spirits (vættir) associated with particular locations, agricultural lands, and animals. These vættir were believed to have been capable of taking on a physical form and were often referred to as landvaettir (land wights) or just vaettir (wights). The word fylgja is itself used to mean "follow" and has been theorized as having a double meaning, with the possible interpretation that it refers both to the "follower" spirit and the guardian spirit of a particular place.

Many of the followers of Norse paganism have been known to have had a fylgja. The practice of having one is known as fylgjusongr, and many medieval Vikings believe that a fylgja or "shadow-sister" may appear when one is in most need of her magical protection, and then she will disappear again when her work is done. That, in itself, indicates the fylgja's role as a guardian from within a spiritual realm.

In the Eddas, there is mention of several kinds of people having a fylgja. They believed that the shadow sister would be the first to notice that their soul was about to leave their body and who decided to give them a sign that she was there. They would take on human form or appear as small animals. In some instances, they are seen as the reincarnation of a dead person. In shamanic terms, the Norse vaettir can be seen as having several roles:

- As guides to the Underworld and guardians of its secrets
- As teachers
- As protectors of certain aspects of life
- As shape-shifters

When a person who is interested in Norse paganism has a fylgja, it is very much like having an animal or force spirit guide who can serve as a powerful protector. These guardian spirits watch over and care for their human counterpart. It has been said that the fylgja can shape shift frequently but will often take on the form of a human, animal, or bird. The word itself refers to the fact that these divine beings serve their human counterparts by helping them to better understand themselves and their role in the world. These sound like poetic descriptions of a personal guardian angel, which is exactly the kind of thing that a fylgja is meant to be.

Like the shaman, the fylgja can be a powerful force in metaphysics and spells. It can add to the strength of such work, offering as much protection as it can when needed. In a situation where someone is being attacked, the fylgja will most likely try to help them or make sure that nothing too dire happens to them.

Nowadays, most people have abandoned this notion, calling it simply superstition. There are no signs or indications of these spirits in our daily lives, so when we hear about these spirits from folklore, we easily disregard them as untruths built to bolster the truth. The fact that these spirits are invisible and not tangible to us makes it that much easier to believe they do not exist anymore.

Interestingly, some still believe in fylgja and still seek them out. Most of them are shamans, but for those who do not practice Shamanism or are unfamiliar with the idea of spirits, a fylgja can be a spiritual guide or companion linked to one's destiny in the same manner as an animal totem would be. There is an almost infinite variety of different fylgja, but most of them fall into certain patterns. Some common patterns can be seen in the characteristics assigned to each fylgja by the local people, and while there are no consistent features among all cultures of what a fylgja looks like, there is a similarity among many beliefs that they appear as spirits or fairies in human form. They may or may not have wings and may sometimes appear as animals. Some common characteristics of fylgja include:

- They appear to a person at a young age, usually before the age of five
- They are always present and provide protection when needed
- Their presence increases in times of danger, illness, or stress
- They can help guide our lives and help us find what we seek
- The fylgja stays with someone until it feels the time has come that they are ready to move on. Then, they will leave the person's side.

Just as there are different ways the fylgja appears in our lives as animals, there are also different reasons why a spirit may choose to become our companion. Some believe that a person's fate can be changed by changing their guardian spirit, while others believe we must grow along with our fylgja instead of trying to change it or make it go away. For example, Native Americans believe you must be ready to die when your fylgja leaves you. Some others associate these spirits with astrology and try to find out which signs or planets are associated with their fylgja. Although some information can be used in this regard, there isn't enough proof that places any importance on astrology when it comes to recognizing a fylgja.

Regardless of how you see your fylgja, contacting them is a great idea to better understand where they come from and what they want. The interaction depends on the person and the spirit, but be aware that not all fylgjas are friendly or good-tempered. If you are having difficulty finding your spirit guide or connecting with them, you may want to seek the help of others who believe in these spirits. They may be able to help you out in some way.

How Can a Fylgja Help You?

A fylgja is a spirit that has identified itself with a person and has come to live with them. It is natural for them to want to be involved in the lives of that person. This can be a good thing if you have someone in your life who will guide you, support you and keep you safe in times of crisis. A fylgja wants us to live our lives as well as we can, and there are several ways it can help us to do so:

- It can contact you when you are in a dangerous situation and provide you with the means to get out of it
- It can help you develop your talents and skills
- It can help you discover important information about yourself
- It can provide you with the guidance you need to find happiness
- It can give you advice about your problems
- It can help you understand what is going on in the world around you
- It can help you understand why someone is angry or upset with you
- It can teach you more about things that have been bothering or confusing you
- It can show you things of interest, including warnings of both good and bad events, letting you know what you need to do to be ready for both instances

While many may not believe in these spirits anymore, they can still be helpful in our lives. The Fylgjur is often seen as a guide or companion, but many people also feel they are good luck charms. This is because of the way we see the fylgja as a representative of a certain type of spirit. They can guide us when we have questions about who we are and our purpose here on Earth. Some even believe that a fylgja brings out our inner self when we need it most, and it is a reminder of our inner nature. There are other beliefs that fylgjur are connected to our personal power and the strength we gain from the universe. It seems to be more like empowerment than a mere guardian spirit who protects us from danger. In fact, it has been said to be our personal connection to the universe, helping us bridge the gap between the world of our spirit guides and the physical world.

Signs That a Fylgja Is Guiding You

There are myriad signs that a fylgja is guiding you, such as:

- Physically, you may be experiencing an increase in luck. Examples include winning the lottery or receiving cash prizes.

- You may be able to enhance your intuition. Your intuition will come in handy if your fylgja is nearby and trying to help you.

- You may be able to make sudden significant changes in your life and get over the situations that were holding you back from succeeding. This change can mean starting a business, getting out of debt, or simply moving where it is more convenient for you and your family.

- You may feel like something you saw was very meaningful. This could be a dream, a conversation, or a new idea you got from someone else. It could also be a message that comes to you through smell and sound.

- You may experience more peace and calm in your life, allowing you to accomplish much more than you would have before the fylgja's arrival. In some cases, fylgja can assist you in the healing process of your past.

- You may have flashes of insight or an epiphany about your life or the world around you without even realizing it at first.

- Some people also see visions or hear voices when their fylgja visits them.

Getting in Touch with Your Fylgja

If you have never seen a fylgja, it is likely because you have never looked for one. Not everyone sees these spirits, as some people choose not to see them or are simply not receptive to this kind of information. For those who believe in the existence of these spirits, there are two ways you can go about finding them; calling upon them or waiting for a sign that they want us to find them.

If you are looking for a spirit guide, there are some things you can do to make things easier on yourself. Before trying to contact them, you should try to find out as much information about them as possible. If you can find out what type of animal or symbol they represent, it may be easier for you to recognize their presence in your life. You may also want to learn more about how a fylgja chooses their human companions and how people were chosen in the past. Reading about how a fylgja has affected the lives of people whose characteristics they seem to match is also helpful.

If you are trying to find your fylgja, you can also try to contact them through meditation or other forms of divination. This can be very helpful in some cases, especially if someone else knows about the spirit you are trying to contact. They can provide support for the connection being made between the worlds. Some spells have been used to attract a fylgja's attention, although these spells haven't been proven to work for everyone.

In the past, people have been able to find their fylgja through dreams or visions. These kinds of experiences were usually very powerful, and people felt that they were given a glimpse into something amazing and beautiful. Although the choice to believe in a fylgja is completely up to you, it can be useful for those seeking a better connection and understanding of their lives.

Calling Upon Your Fylgja

If you have determined that it is time for you to find a fylgja and establish a connection, there are some steps you can follow to get their attention.

Step 1: You'll need to find the fylgja. You'll have to look for signs that a fylgja is guiding you, and this is where the information above about identifying your fylgja can really help. Adopting a kind of mindset that will help you connect with them is also useful. Once you have decided to look for your fylgja, you need to be on the lookout for signs that they are around. Sometimes these signs can be as simple as seeing a bird or hearing a strange noise. It's also a good idea to keep an eye out for premonitions or even dreams and visions about what your fylgja may look like.

Step 2: Call upon the spirit guide to make itself known. There are different ways of calling upon your fylgja, and it's up to you to decide which way is best for you. Some people like to make offerings and sacrifices to their fylgja so that they will know how much you value them. Other people like to keep a special space with pictures or mementos of the animal or symbol they think represents their fylgja. This can help identify your spirit guide when they are ready to make contact.

Step 3: After doing these two things, it is time for you to sit back and wait for your fylgja to make its presence known. It may be hard not to try to force the connection, but remember that it is up to them if they want you to see them or not, and whether you see them, they are still there, guiding and helping you. The more time you spend trying to connect with them, the more sensitive you'll be to their presence, and the easier it will be for you to notice their signature in your life.

FAQ

Q: Should I only be calling on a particular fylgja, or can I call on several fylgjur?

A: It is up to you to decide if you'll call on one fylgja or multiple fylgjurs. They can come in all shapes and sizes, and different people may have different types of connections with different ones. If you are having difficulty with the connection, it may be beneficial to stay connected to one particular guide who seems to fit your situation the best.

Q: Can I have more than one Fylgja?

A: Yes, you can have more than one Fylgja, although this is not always the case for particular individuals. If you are drawing on two different Fylgjur symbols that aren't necessarily related to each other in some way, then it may be possible to have two different guides. It's also worth pointing out that maybe your first guide was just keeping your attention while they waited for something they thought was more compatible with your energy.

Q: How can I always keep my Fylgja close to me?

A: This is a very important question since a Fylgja is something you'll have with you for the rest of your life. It is helpful to have an object you can use to connect with your Fylgja. A pendant, necklace, or ring can be used as a totem or charm to remind you of your guide. You can also use this object to seek guidance from them when they are not immediately present.

Q: What if my fylgja is not a certain animal or symbol?

A: This is a very common question, and it is important to make sure that you are looking in the right direction. Everyone has a different belief system and a different way of seeing the world, but certain symbols can still represent the same thing. The question you want to ask yourself is, "What does this remind me of?" Once you recognize the connection, it can be easier to pick out the fylgja's presence in your life.

Chapter Nine: How to Journey through the Realms

This chapter is specifically written to teach you how to journey through the lower, middle, and higher realms. This is an extremely important and sacred experience for many people and is becoming popular as more people seek out shamanic practices. To journey into realms, you need to be in a meditative state where your mind is clear and calm. There are a few ways to achieve this, but the easiest is to use the techniques I have described in previous chapters.

For the lower realm, your intention for this journey must be something that will help you gain knowledge from your experience or find closure on an issue, so it can pass from your life (or, as shamans like to say, the energy moves on). For the middle realm, the intent should be to have a beneficial experience that will help you in your life. You could also use this time for healing or even starting a new career or other projects. For the higher realms, we usually do this for enlightenment (or, as some people call it, "heaven"). Also, you must ensure your protection and the protection of your space before you even attempt any of these exercises. More information on cleansing and protection will be available in the next chapter.

The Lower Realm

This realm can be a very intense experience and should not be attempted by someone mentally unstable, as it is filled with a great deal of emotional energy. However, it can be very powerful to help you gain knowledge if you're not afraid of the experience. The lower realm represents the subconscious or unconscious mind. It operates at a different frequency and does not function as part of the reality we are normally aware of. It is designed the same way our physical brain is designed, processing information and storing it for later use. In shamanic terms, anything that could be a mental block, emotional trauma, or negative belief system is stored in the lower realms. It is essentially a part of us that looks like a dream (or trance) state but is still in existence and doing what it needs to do. The subconscious mind creates images that can be as mundane or strange as you want them to be (as with dreams), and we use them to create thoughts and intentions that are later used consciously when we become fully aware of them.

Journey through the Lower Realm

This journey is made to learn about your subconscious mind, cleanse it of any negativity, and heal yourself from any trauma you may be holding on to there. It is a very fast-paced experience and often only lasts a few minutes. If you intend to use any entheogens, only do so under the watchful guidance of a seasoned shaman. If not, you can use the following exercises to get your journey started and gain some insight into yourself.

It begins by going into a deep meditative state. You can, if you want, begin by going into a light trance, but most people choose to go straight into a deep trance. When you are in this deep meditative state, you should be fully conscious of what is happening around you, but most of your conscious mind should be blocked out to experience your subconscious. This way, your subconscious mind can fully control what it does with the information it receives from your conscious mind.

When you are ready and have settled in, imagine a place in nature that could take you lower, like a volcano, cave, or even the ocean. The point here is to go downward. When you are in this place, you'll feel a pull, which means that your mind wants you to go down into the depths of your subconscious. Don't resist the pull. Let yourself be pulled into the depths.

When you reach the ground of your subconscious mind, imagine a tunnel opening up in front of you that leads even further downward. Walk down into this tunnel and follow it as it takes you deeper and deeper into the darkness of your mind. If there are any obstacles in this place or anything that tries to stop you from going further, do not stop and struggle with them. Just step around them, over them, or act as if they were not there. You are now going deeper into the subconscious mind than you would ever have imagined possible.

As you get deeper into the tunnel, you'll find that the walls of this tunnel start to become much lighter and more translucent. This is because you have already gone so far inside your subconscious that it gets easier and easier to see what lies on the other side of these walls. Soon enough, a light will come toward you. This is your spirit animal and can be found in this realm. Do not try to stop this light. Let yourself be pulled forward as it takes you on your journey further into your subconscious. Take note of the things you see and hear and the sensations you feel as you travel. These are all memories and experiences stored in your subconscious mind, and they will be clues as to which choices you'll make in the future.

At the end of your journey, you'll find a door. This door is a gateway that goes through to your conscious mind, and you should open it and pass through it. You must come back to your conscious mind. You cannot stay in your subconscious indefinitely. You'll know when you pass through the doorway because you'll immediately feel different.

Your subconscious mind is much more connected to your body than your conscious mind is. Part of this journey is to discover why you have certain feelings, ideas, or even urges and to understand why you do certain things. You now have the opportunity to go through the rest of your subconscious and explore more of what it has stored away. This will help you better understand yourself and will give you more information on where your destiny lies.

The Middle Realm

The middle realm represents the conscious mind, and it is here that we experience our reality. This realm is all about experiencing your emotions, whether they are negative or positive. It is here where you decide what you feel and who you are. The middle realms are the most important in shamanic practice because the purpose of all the journeys and techniques we do is to help us better understand ourselves and control our minds.

When you enter the conscious mind, you are now ready to become aware of your emotions. You may notice that everything feels different, and you have a much stronger connection with your body. Suddenly, it is much easier for you to sense what your body wants or needs. You can feel when your muscles ache or when anything else is wrong with them. Your conscious mind will experience an intense connection with your emotions and sensations because it has forgotten about them over time. In this realm, you'll experience yourself at full capacity.

Journey through the Middle Realm

When ready, go to a place representing your conscious mind. Some say this place is like a small village or perhaps a cabin in the woods. This place is different for everyone, but it should represent somewhere you feel safe, comfortable, and at home. It should also represent your true self, your personality, and how you think the world works. Your mind will be very open to suggestions in this place, so you must spend as much time and energy on creating the perfect setting.

When you are ready and settled, imagine that you are floating in the air, high above where you are. You should be aware of your surroundings but not feel pressured to look down at them or be afraid of what you see. Look at everything you see, but stay conscious of what you are looking at. As you look at each thing, tell yourself that you are seeing it right now and that nothing will change. This is important because if you doubt these things or think they will change while in the middle realm, your subconscious mind will do its best to make them change. You must know that everything stays the same and will always stay the same.

Now bring yourself back down to the ground where everything else lives. This can be done by imagining falling from a great height until your feet hit the ground in a place that represents your conscious mind. You may feel a rush of energy as you fall, which is a sign that you have successfully made it to the Middle Realm. You are now free to explore and observe the things that make up your reality. Look around at all of your surroundings. What do you see? What do you smell? What do you feel? Not only is this place a representation of where you are in life, but it is also a representation of who you are. Are the walls made of wood or stone? Are there windows or sunlight streaming through them? If there are people in this place, who are they, and what is their relationship to your conscious mind? All of these things are important because they represent our psyche and how we perceive the world around us.

There is no wrong way to make this journey. The point is to go through the middle realm and note everything in it. Be careful not to change anything here, or bring new things into your conscious mind that you did not already have there. Just observe everything with an open mind and a clear heart. This journey can be made alone or with assistance from a shamanic practitioner who can give you more details about what you see and what it means. You should observe the people and relationships in your mind because they will show your relationships with yourself, others, and your spirit guides.

When you have finished your journey, you should be able to answer questions such as "Is everything in my conscious mind the way I would like it to be?" or "Are there any relationships that need to change?" Anytime you finish a journey, getting back in touch with your body is important. This can be as simple as scratching your hand or as complex as a hug from a loved one.

The Higher Realm

The higher realm is the spiritual world that we are connected to. It is here where our spirit guides and ancestors live. It is a world where anything is possible, and the rules of our reality do not necessarily apply just yet. Sometimes this realm can be challenging because we have to learn how to balance and control our emotions. However, it is also here where you'll discover your purpose for being on Earth at this time and what needs to be learned for you to achieve your full potential in life.

Journey through The Higher Realm

Many people are exploring the higher realm at this time, but it can be a very difficult place to access. Shamans have been journeying here for thousands of years and better understand how to reach this place successfully. However, this journey is new and uncharted territory for most of us. This journey can only be made with the assistance of a shamanic practitioner. You should also be prepared for this to be a challenging journey, but it will be worth the effort.

When you are ready, find a place representing your spirit guides and/or ancestors. Every culture has its own imagery for this realm, so the more time you spend researching their history, the better the representation will be. This should be a place that feels open and free since you can explore everything here. There should also be different creatures that are part of the spiritual realm, including your spirit guides and ancestors. If you have any items that represent these things, it may help if you take them with you on your journey. Again, make sure everything is safe for you to handle because, in this realm, anything can happen.

When ready, enter a meditative state leading you into a trance. During this meditation, imagine a place in nature that can take you upward. This can be the "world tree," a staircase, a ball of smoke, or even a whirlwind. As you go up, make sure that you can feel the different elements surrounding you as you travel. It is normal to experience a transition into the realm of the spirits; this can be understood as the threshold of what you know and what you don't know. When you cross this threshold, feel yourself become lighter and lighter until there is no longer a sense of body. You are now coming into the spirit realm. This is your chance to explore and take in all of the sights and sensations that come to you.

The trick to this journey is to be open-minded and free of any preconceived ideas about what the place looks like or how it should look. Don't think about these things because your subconscious mind will make them happen. You should just allow yourself to be open to the possibilities of what you can see and experience. If this is your first time on this journey, you may become overwhelmed or overstimulated until you learn how things work here. Do not be surprised if you see entities or spirits that are related to you or the place where your body is currently at. Everything you see can have a purpose for why it is here, but you may have to delve into your subconscious mind later to find the answers. If anything feels scary or overwhelming during this journey, it is important to calm down and try to connect with your spirit guides and ancestors. They will be able to guide you back into the world of the living when necessary. When you have finished your journey, you can come back by moving down a tunnel of light until your feet touch the ground. Then open your eyes and become re-rooted on the Earth with all of its elements.

Chapter Ten: Shamanic Self-Care and Protection

Many people practice spiritual self-care and protection, but not everyone knows how to do it effectively, which is completely understandable. It's difficult for those who don't have a shamanic background to understand the protections they need and how to implement them. This last chapter will guide you on how to cleanse yourself, your environment, and even things such as your space, energies, tools, or objects confidently using shamanic cleansing and protection practices.

Cleansing is one of the best ways to prevent being held hostage by negativity in your life and in your surroundings. You don't have to be the victim of other people's problems anymore. You can rise above them and protect yourself, your family, and even your friends against negative energies and spirits. For those who aren't familiar with the concept of spiritual cleansing, it basically entails removing all negative entities or forces attached to a given place or object (or oneself) through cleansing ceremonies, rituals, or spells.

What Are Negative Entities?

Negative entities are those evil spirits, ghosts, and other unpleasant energies that dwell in the world. The more negativity you encounter, the more you'll need to cleanse yourself spiritually to prevent it from affecting your life. This may sound a bit like magic and paranormal witchcraft, but it's actually not as complicated as people make it out to be.

You don't need supernatural powers or big rituals to purge or banish negative energies. All you need is proper cleansing practices and protection methods to keep them away.

The Importance of Shamanic Cleansing and Protection

Shamanic cleansing and protection are of paramount importance when it comes to spirits and entities, but especially when it comes to negative energies. It's just as important to cleanse yourself and make sure you remove negative energies from your life as it is to protect yourself from these spirits. After a successful shamanic journey, the shaman might bring back aspects of the journey with them, and they can be affected by the negative energies that come along with these spirits. You see, entities and energy have a way of sticking around for a long time if proper cleansing and protection are not performed afterward. This is why cleansing is of utmost importance, especially in the shamanic practice.

Clearing the clutter before and after engaging in any kind of shamanic journey lets you focus on what matters. It opens up your channels to allow positive energy and spirits to enter while banishing negative energies and entities from your space. You might think that cleansing or protection is just a 'new-age' practice, but it has actually been a vital part of all ancient spiritual practices. Even ancient shamans believed in external and internal cleansing to protect themselves against negativity affecting their journeys, rituals, healing practices, and day-to-day life.

Although cleansing your space and energies is a great way to eliminate negative entities, it's also a great way to cleanse yourself spiritually and mentally. Insidious negative voices might get stuck in your head, preventing you from taking action. If you've ever suffered from negativity in your life, you probably know what it's like to feel demoralized and unmotivated by the mundane day-to-day tasks of your life. Once you start cleansing your space and yourself, these negative energies get pushed out, and the voices of motivation start coming back to you, giving you the energy to work through whatever problems are in your way.

Methods to Achieve a Spiritual Cleanse

Shamanic cleansing rituals can basically be done in a variety of ways. To ensure you're appropriately performing the rituals, you must follow certain guidelines and instructions when conducting them. A cleansing ritual could range from simple prayers and meditations to full-blown ceremonies involving drumming, dancing, chanting, burning sacred herbs, and even consuming hallucinogenic plants in some cultures. Whatever the method, you should feel good about it and not feel forced or obligated to do it against your will or belief. A few cleansing methods include:

Washing: One of the best ways to cleanse yourself is to use good old-fashioned washing. Most people do not realize that washing your space or surrounding objects is a traditional practice. When you tidy up your room, wash dishes, or keep your living space clean and orderly, you're essentially purifying your body, spirit, and environment from negative energies. Washing, in this sense, encompasses more than just taking a shower. You can also cleanse by letting the water flow over you, imitating rain pouring down on you. Water is a great cleanser of spirits and entities and is one of the easiest ways to cleanse yourself. Shamanic cleansing with water is simple, effective, and cheap.

Smudging: Smudging is a traditional practice most people are familiar with from eastern traditions. You'll need smudge sticks, which you can buy or make yourself to perform smudging. Simply take a smudge stick, light it up and pass the smoke around yourself or your space. This is a great way to remove negative energies from your home and yourself while attracting positive ones. It's also one of the best ways to ritually cleanse your body and spirit together. For a DIY smudge stick, you'll need sage, but you can also make use of other herbs like lavender, cedar, etc. If you're not sure what kind of herbs to use, go with sage or lavender, as they are traditionally used for smudging. When you have the dried herbs, tie them together with a string or use a traditional leather cord to make a long smudge stick.

Sweeping: Another way to remove negative energies from your person or environment is through sweeping. It is an excellent way to banish negative entities and cleanse yourself without feeling too ceremonial about it. To perform a sweeping cleanse, you'll need to get a broom, preferably one made from natural fibers such as straw or palm fibers. Clean your space with the broom to expel any negative forces or entities. Use it in conjunction with another cleansing ritual, like smudging, for a stronger effect.

Using Crystals: Crystals have been used for centuries to harness the power of healing and cleansing. They can be very effective in achieving a more spiritual cleanse because they positively affect your mind and body. Crystals like amethyst or selenite are known to deflect negative energy from yourself and the environment. Quartz crystals are also great for this purpose, as are tourmalines, topaz, and jasper. Carry them with you or place them strategically in your living space to make all the difference.

Sunlight: Harnessing the sun's power is a powerful way to achieve spiritual cleansing. Sunlight purifies everything it touches and can be used to get rid of negative entities as well. Simply go outside at a time when the sun is strong, sit quietly and get yourself cleansed by the power of the sun. You can also place items that need cleansing in sunlight so that they can be purified and protected by it.

Breathing Techniques: You can also use breathing techniques like pranayama to purify yourself and your space. Pranayama is a technique used in yoga that involves breathing exercises that involve controlling the breath so that it becomes deep, slow, and rhythmic. It has many benefits, especially when it comes to eliminating toxins from your system. You can use this power while performing shamanic rituals as a way of purification.

Using Salt: Salt has been used for centuries by diverse cultures as a way to purify one's body and soul. Its powerful cleansing abilities are well documented, and you can harness them in your shamanic practice. To cleanse yourself with salt, light an incense stick (preferably one made from natural plant matter), and get a bowl of salt. Sit quietly and meditate as you let the incense smoke waft over your body. Now, imagine the smoke is purifying you and removing any internal negative energies or entities. When you've finished, pour the salt into a bowl of water and pour it over your head and let it stream down the rest of your body. Or, you can dip your hands in the bowl of salt water and wash your face with it.

Protection Rituals

Protection rituals are an important part of shamanism, particularly when you're dealing with spirits, activities, or locations that are supposed to be harmful or known to attract dangerous spirits. Shamanism is a tradition that requires you to be very careful while performing rituals, as they often involve elements and forces that can be potentially hazardous if handled wrong. You'll need to use special methods and tools to keep yourself safe during your spiritual practice, even if it's just something as simple as making sure you don't accidentally summon an evil spirit while performing a purification ritual. Protection rituals can be used to protect you on your spiritual journey and make it easier for you to navigate the path of shamanism. There are various ways to protect yourself against unwanted spirits and entities. A few of these ways include:

The Power of Imagination: The power of your imagination is very strong and can help protect yourself against spirits. You can use this power to imagine your spirit body as a powerful warrior that is impenetrable by outside forces. You can also use this power to conjure a protective shield around yourself or your space that repels any negative energies or entities that may try to attack you. You'll need to use your senses, imagination, and spirit mind to do this. Visualize the space you're in, feeling the air around you and sensing your surroundings. Realize that all of these elements are part of your spirit body and that they are a part of you by nature. Use them in tandem to create a protective shield around yourself or your space at times when you feel vulnerable or are preparing to embark on a shamanic journey.

Using Essential Oils: Essential oils like frankincense, myrrh, and bergamot are known to have the power that can protect your spirit and body. They can be used in protection rituals to repel negative forces. For example, you could mix three drops of each of these oils and clean water in a glass bottle and spray it on yourself or your space. This will be enough to keep away any harmful spirits, but if you want to make things more effective, add another essential oil like sage or birch to the mixture.

Using Amulets: Amulets have been used since ancient times to keep negative forces, entities, and spirits away. They can be made from different materials, but the most popular ones are made from silver or stone. You can also find them in other materials such as wood, metal, etc. Amulets can be worn around the neck or wrist – or even held in your hand during rituals or shamanic practices.

Using Chants: There are certain chants you can use to keep yourself safe during your spiritual journey. They work by repelling harmful spirits and consequently keeping you safe from them. Chants are often derived from ancient prayers and mantras that were believed to repel evil spirits, hence their effectiveness in protection rituals today. You can adopt these chants as your own and use them when you feel you're under attack from evil spirits.

Using a Drum: In the ancient traditions of shamanism, the beating of drums was used to drive away spirits and negative influences. The rhythm of the drum is also said to be therapeutic and relaxes anyone listening to it. You can use this power to keep yourself safe from outside forces. Beat a traditional drum and let its rhythm calm your mind and body. The beating of the drum will also protect you during your spiritual journey, as the sound is a powerful repellent for outside forces.

Using Totems: Totems are items that are used in shamanic rites to help in purification and protection. They can be animals like snakes and owls or stones (like crystals and gemstones). Remember that you'll need to choose your totem wisely. It's a good idea to choose one that represents your spirit body and resonates with you the most. You can use this totem to repel evil spirits or ask for protection during your spiritual practice.

Using Food and Drink: Food and drink can be used in protection rituals as a tool for purifying yourself. After performing a cleansing ritual, you can use food and drink to protect yourself from bad spirits and negative energies. Some foods that are known to help in purification are pecan nuts, cranberries, green tea, elderflowers, apple cider vinegar, and many others. You could also add garnishing of rosemary or sage to your food or drink tea made from herbs of protection such as peppermint, bay leaves, and basil.

Using Crystal Grids: Crystals can be used in protection rituals for two reasons. Firstly, to create a protective shield around one's self and space, and secondly, to collect and transform negative energy into positive energy. The first way requires hanging crystals from your neck or placing them in your home so that they form a protective grid. The second way requires you to create a crystal grid and then perform a ritual in front of it. To create a crystal grid, you'll need to place crystals of the same energy around each other, preferably in a sacred geometrical shape. The most popular of these shapes include a circle, square, triangle, pentagon, and hexagon. You can use quartz, citrine, or amethyst crystals for this purpose.

Banishing Ritual

The purpose of a banishing ritual is to remove unwanted people, issues, and influences from the person or space it protects. These unwanted influences are often negative energies and entities that may be harming the person or may be causing the person to suffer – in such cases, a banishing ritual will be used to remove them and keep them away. To perform a simple banishing ritual, follow these steps:

1. Sprinkle sage or cedar around all four corners of the room or space. This will help to clear away negative energies in the area and open it for traditional cleansing. Use salt or sea salt instead if no sage or cedar is available.

2. Invoke the purpose of the ritual and state that you wish to banish any harmful spirits or entities in the area.

3. Light a candle and demand that the negative force or forces leave.

4. Blow out all the candles.

5. Cleanse the area with water and sprinkle salt over it to clear out any residue.

Conclusion

Norse Shamanism is a fascinating topic. It exposes the beliefs and ways of life of the Norse people during the Viking Age. Unfortunately, its vastness and lack of modern understanding make it difficult to form cohesive thoughts about what it really means. With no central books or texts, we can only turn to other sources, such as bedtime stories and myths, to get information about this culture.

In this book, we have presented observations on Norse Shamanism while examining their cosmological view in comparison with our own day-to-day lives in an attempt to paint a picture that is both accurate and meaningful for current times as well as for generations past.

Throughout this book, we have hopefully encouraged you to think, consider and imagine the possibilities that may exist beyond our daily lives. This book is not meant to be a guide for practicing Norse Shamanism per se but rather an attempt to uncover some of the more pragmatic pockets of this culture and its cosmology.

Many aspects of this practice are left for the reader to ponder. Please accept it as a stimulus for thought and imagination. It's never too late to learn more about the history and practice of Norse Shamanism. One day, you may even consider becoming a true shaman yourself, but for now, consider this your introduction to the subject and the path to your own imagination. Think of your journey as one of discovery, and allow your intuition to guide you on how you'd like to make Norse shamanism a practical thing in your daily life. If this is your chosen path, you'll find it infinitely rewarding.

Here's another book by Silvia Hill that you might like

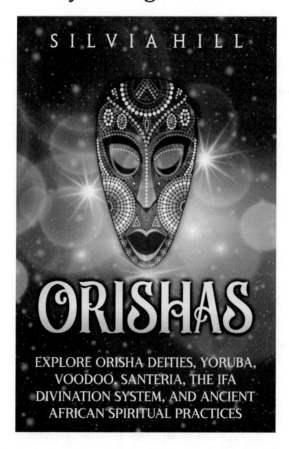

Free Bonus from Silvia Hill available for limited time

Hi Spirituality Lovers!

My name is Silvia Hill, and first off, I want to THANK YOU for reading my book.

Now you have a chance to join my exclusive spirituality email list so you can get the ebooks below for free as well as the potential to get more spirituality ebooks for free! Simply click the link below to join.

P.S. Remember that it's 100% free to join the list.

~~$27~~ FREE BONUSES

 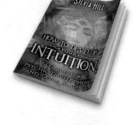

- 9 Types of Spirit Guides and How to Connect to Them
- How to Develop Your Intuition: 7 Secrets for Psychic Development and Tarot Reading
- Tarot Reading Secrets for Love, Career, and General Messages

Access your free bonuses here
https://livetolearn.lpages.co/norse-shamanism-paperback/

References

Andren, Anders, and Kristina Jennbert. 2006. Old Norse Religion In Long-Term Perspectives. Chicago: Nordic Academic Press.

Andrén, Anders, Kristina Jennbert, and Catharina Raudvere. 2006. Old Norse Religion In Long-Term Perspectives. Lund: Nordic Academic Press.

Boekhoven, Jeroen W. 2011. Genealogies Of Shamanism. Groningen: Barkhuis.

Brink, Nicholas E. n.d. Baldr's Magic.

Kaldera, Raven, and Galina Krasskova. n.d. Neolithic Shamanism.

Kaldera, Raven. 2006. Northern-Tradition Shamanism. Hubbardston, Mass.: Asphodel Press.

Lindow, John. n.d. Old Norse Mythology.

Ollhoff, Jim. 2011. Norse Mythology. Edina, Minn.: ABDO Pub. Co.

Tolley, Clive. 2009. Shamanism In Norse Myth And Magic. Helsinki: Suomalainen Tiedeakatemia.

Chaline, Eric. 2004. The Book Of Gods & Goddesses. New York: HarperEntertainment.

Einarsson, Stefan, and Jean I. Young. 1956. "The Prose Edda Of Snorri Sturluson". Modern Language Notes 71 (5): 393. doi:10.2307/3043466.

Francis, Paul. 2017. The Shamanic Journey. [Place of publication not identified]: Paul Francis.

Gregg, Susan. 2005. Dance Of Power. Mountain View, HI: I.M. Pub.

Hughes-Calero, Heather. 1994. The Shamanic Journey Living As Soul. Sedona, Ariz.: Higher Consciousness Books.

Smith, Ryan. n.d. The Way Of Fire And Ice.

v. Schnurbein, Stefanie. 2003. "Shamanism In The Old Norse Tradition: A Theory Between Ideological Camps." History Of Religions 43 (2): 116-138. doi:10.1086/423007

Made in the USA
Thornton, CO
12/18/24 20:48:52

0116c781-94b8-4ca6-86bb-0f4838bc9a9eR01